FAST TRACK ENGLISH

Focus on
Words and Phrases

Robert Parr

MMD
MULTIMEDIA DIENSTLEISTUNGEN
Nürnberg MMD GmbH

Multimedia-Dienstleistungen Nürnberg MMD GmbH

Die Deutsche Bibliothek – CIP-Einheitsaufnahme

Fast track English [Medienkombination] / Rober Parr. - Nürnberg: MMD
Focus on words and phrases. - 1999

3. Auflage 2007

Zeichnungen: Daniel Schwarz, Köln (S. 10, S. 30)
Umschlaggestaltung: Franziska Schob-Bergmeir, München
Gesamtherstellung: Gebr. Bremberger GmbH & Co. KG, Unterschleißheim

Vorwort

Die Bedeutung des Wortschatzes beim Erlernen einer Fremdsprache wird oft unterschätzt. Dabei ist er doch der Grundstock einer jeden Sprache. Auch die besten Grammatikkenntnisse helfen nichts, hat man im wahrsten Sinne des Wortes „nichts zu sagen". Mit einem soliden Reservoir an Wörtern und Redewendungen ist man hingegen bald in der Lage, sich an einem Gespräch zu beteiligen.

Natürlich kommt es beim erfolgreichen „Wörterlernen" immer auf den richtigen Kontext an. Wer sich Buchstabe für Buchstabe mühsam durchs Alphabet arbeitet, stur einzelne Vokabeln ohne jeden Anwendungsbezug „paukt", wird immer wieder feststellen, hängengeblieben ist eigentlich wenig, und will man das Wenige voller Stolz anwenden, ist es häufig der falsche Zusammenhang.

Focus on Words and Phrases beschäftigt sich vorwiegend mit dem Wortschatz aus den drei *Fast Track*-Bänden - *Part One*, *Part Two* und *The Business World.* Das Buch enthält 50 thematisch gegliederte *units*, die aus je einer Doppelseite bestehen. Die linke Seite führt in ein Wortschatzfeld ein, z.B. *family and friends*, *money matters* oder *sport*. Auf der rechten Seite folgt der dazugehörige Übungsteil.

Es ist nicht ratsam, die *units* der Reihe nach durchzuarbeiten. Sie sollten sich eher die Gebiete aussuchen, die Sie jeweils besonders interessieren. Lesen Sie sich zunächst die linke Seite genau durch. Machen Sie sich mit Hilfe eines einsprachigen Wörterbuchs und der zweisprachigen *wordlist* aus dem Anhang eigene Notizen zu Ihnen unbekannten Wörtern und Wendungen.

Bei der Zusammenstellung dieser *wordlist* wurde aus der Vielzahl der *words and phrases* bewußt eine Auswahl getroffen. Sie beinhaltet fast ausschließlich wichtige Begriffe der linken Seiten, d.h. der Erklärteile. Im Anhang finden Sie auch Lösungsvorschläge zu den Übungsteilen.

And now over to you!

Robert Parr

Contents

1 About dictionaries (I)

A. A good dictionary can help you to learn new words. It can tell you …

- what a word **means**
- which **part of speech** it belongs to
- which **grammatical features** it has
- how to **combine** it with other words
- what it means in your **first language**
- how to **pronounce** it
- how to **stress** it
- how to **spell** it
- how **formal** or **informal** it is
- if it's **British** or **US English**

B. Words often have **more** than one meaning.

There was a terrible jam on the way to work this morning.
Would you like some jam with your toast?

C. Words **combine** with other words. For example, it makes sense to learn the word 'pie' in combination with 'shepherd's' or the word 'lamb' in combination with 'chops'.

They serve traditional food like shepherd's pie.
They also offer lamb chops.

D. A good dictionary contains a lot of words to describe language. Here, for example, are some words which name **parts of speech**.

part of speech	example	part of speech	example
adjective	red, difficult	adverb	slowly, well
article	a, the	conjunction	and, but
gerund	seeing, winning	infinitive	to go, to hear
noun	student, mother	preposition	in, at
pronoun	she, him	verb	writes, had

E. A good dictionary contains information about **word building**. Look at the word 'comfort'.

root	prefix	suffix	adjective
comfort	un-	-able	uncomfortable

1 Practice

I. Have you got a good monolingual dictionary? Is it one of these?

- ❐ Collins Cobuild English Language Dictionary
- ❐ Longman Dictionary of Contemporary English
- ❐ Oxford Advanced Learner's Dictionary

II. Look up these words in your dictionary. Define them or think of an example sentence to show their meaning.

- ◆ almond
- ◆ garlic
- ◆ flour

III. Look more closely at the dictionary entry for 'garlic'. What do the 'n' and the '[U]' mean?

garlic /ˈgɑːlɪk/ n [U] onion-like plant with strong taste and smell, used in cooking: a clove of ~

IV. Look up the pronunciation of these two words in your dictionary.

- ◆ flour
- ◆ flower

V. What are the German equivalents for this English word? Check in your dictionary.

- ◆ diet

VI. Link the beginnings (1-4) and ends (a-d) of the words to form four things you eat.

1. baked	a. cream
2. boiled	b. potato
3. ice	c. crumble
4. apple	d. egg

VII. Look at the underlined words in this sentence. Which parts of speech are they?

I <u>enjoy</u> reading English <u>books</u> <u>but</u> I don't like <u>speaking</u> English.

2 About dictionaries (II)

A. A good dictionary will show you how to pronounce a word. However, the **phonetic alphabet** contains some unusual **symbols**. It is helpful if you know them.

θ	= 'th' as in	'thick'
ð	= 'th' as in	'they'
dʒ	= 'j' as in	'jam'
tʃ	= 'ch' as in	'church'
ʃ	= 's' as in	'treasure'
æ	= 'a' as in	'man'
ɔ:	= 'o' as in	'born'
ɜ:	= 'i' as in	'bird'
ɒ	= 'o' as in	'stop'
ʊ	= 'u' as in	'put'
ə	= 'a' as in	'about'
ʌ	= 'u' as in	'up'

B. It is important to be able to stress a word properly. (See Unit 42.) In most dictionaries a small mark (ˈ) shows the **main stress**. Another mark (ˌ) shows the **secondary stress**. The mark is always put **before** the stressed **syllable**.

hotel /həʊˈtel/ August /ˈɔ:gəst/
machine /məˈʃi:n/ photographer /ˌfəˈtɒgrəfə/

C. A good dictionary will also tell you if a word is **formal** or **informal**. Many informal words, for example, are **short forms** of longer words.

formal	informal
refrigerator	fridge
advertisement	ad

D. **Formal language** is often found in **notices** or **business correspondence**.

formal	informal
CAR PARK OPEN FOR PATRONS ONLY	only people who are going to come into the pub can use the pub car park
We regret to inform you that you were not successful in your application ...	we are sorry to say that we gave somebody else the job

2 Practice

I. Which words are these? Write them down.

1. /ɔːlˈðəʊ/
2. /ˌkʌp əv ˈtiː/
3. /geɪm/
4. /ˈfɜːnɪtʃə/
5. /peɪdʒ/
6. /ˈsɪzəz/
7. /ˈstʌmək/
8. /ˈtræfɪk ˌdʒæm/

II. Say these words out loud. How many syllables are there? Which one takes the main stress?

1. binoculars
2. capacity
3. fashionable
4. greenhouse
5. muscle
6. unless
7. vegetables
8. vineyard

III. Write down the informal form of these words.

	formal	informal
1.	bicycle	...
2.	telephone	...
3.	newspaper	...
4.	goodbye	...
5.	laboratory	...

IV. Can you say what these notices mean in more informal language?

	formal	informal
1.	KINDLY REFRAIN FROM SMOKING IN THIS THEATRE	...
2.	PENALTY FOR DROPPING LITTER £200	...
3.	SHOPLIFTERS WILL BE PROSECUTED	...
4.	FEEDING THE HORSES IS STRICTLY PROHIBITED	...

3 Advice on learning new words

A. Learning new words is more than learning what they mean. It's also important to know **how to use** them **in combination** with other words.

B. If you want to **remember** new words it may be helpful to put them into **meaningful groups**. Here are three ways of grouping words.

- **a network:**

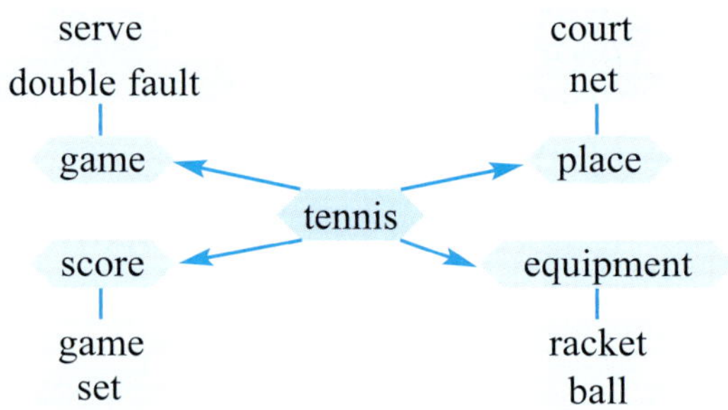

- **a grid:**

	a cake	a mistake	homework	a handstand	a photocopy
to make	✓	✓	x	x	✓
to do	x	x	✓	✓	✓

- **a fork:**

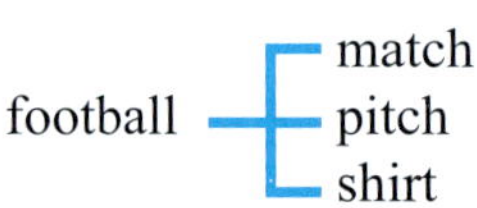

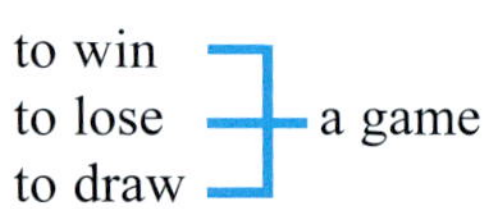

C. Some people can remember words more easily if they do a simple **drawing**.

a shuttlecock

ankle

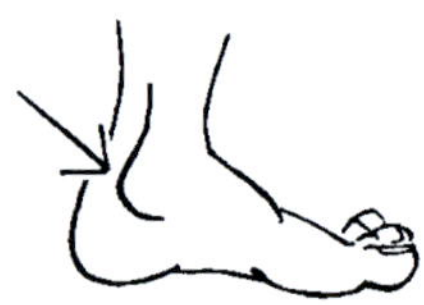

3 Practice

I. What's the best way of remembering a new word? Which of these ideas do you personally find useful?

- writing down the word in a complete sentence
- writing down the word with a translation
- writing down the word with a synonym
- writing down the word with an antonym (opposite)
- writing down the word in another word class (eg noun, adjective, verb)
- writing down the word in a network, grid, fork
- writing down the word with a picture or diagram

II. Now try this short quiz. Mark the correct answer.

1. How many words are there in the English language?
   a) 100,000 and more b) 500,000 and more

2. How many words does an educated English-speaking person know?
   a) about 50,000 b) about 5,000

3. How many words does an educated English-speaking person use in everyday speech?
   a) 500 b) 5,000

4. How many words make up 45% of everything spoken in English?
   a) 1,000 b) 100

What does this quiz tell you about learning new words?

III. When revising new words you may want to think about these ideas.

- you can't - and don't need to - know all the words in the English language
- it's best to learn words that you yourself think are important
- it's easier to learn two lists of 10 words than one list of 20 words
- make learning words an active process by putting them in a meaningful context

4 Basics

A. It's difficult to say what **'basic' vocabulary** is. In the following grid, for example, you can see the **50 most frequent word forms** which occur in a spoken corpus of 200 million words.

no	word forms	frequency	no	word forms	frequency
1.	…	500843	26.	have	84294
2.	…	463445	27.	he	79137
3.	…	367221	28.	for	77842
4.	…	359144	29.	do	77207
5.	it	313032	30.	well	75287
6.	to	308438	31.	think	74543
7.	that	284422	32.	right	74191
8.	a	273009	33.	be	66492
9.	of	242811	34.	this	65424
10.	in	187523	35.	like	63948
11.	er*	178464	36.	've	63160
12.	yeah	155259	37.	at	62654
13.	they	135084	38.	with	61289
14.	was	133022	39.	no	60885
15.	erm*	132836	40.	as	58871
16.	we	124928	41.	mean	58825
17.	mm*	122674	42.	all	58360
18.	is	113420	43.	're	57131
19.	know	111741	44.	or	56857
20.	but	100648	45.	if	56774
21.	so	91836	46.	about	56321
22.	what	89364	47.	not	56109
23.	there	88938	48.	just	55329
24.	on	88456	49.	one	55189
25.	yes	87211	50.	can	53090

* These are 'hesitating noises'.

B. Do you know the **days of the week** in English?

Monday • Tuesday • Wednesday • Thursday • Friday • Saturday • Sunday

C. And the **months of the year**?

January • February • March • April • May • June • July • August
September • October • November • December

4 Practice

I. Section A shows the 50 most common words in spoken English. These make up 35% of everything that is spoken. Which are the first four words missing in the grid? Choose one of the lists below.

list 1	list 2	list 3	list 4
tomato	went	the	July
people	fall	I	CD
school	bye	and	warm
beer	father	you	child

II. Complete the sentences. Use the words in the box.

black ◆ blue ◆ red ◆ white ◆ yellow

1. Black and … make grey.
2. Yellow and … make green.
3. Red and … make brown.
4. Red and … make pink.
5. Blue and … make purple.
6. Red and … make orange.

III. Do you know Solomon Grundy?

Solomon Grundy
Born on Monday
Christened on Tuesday
Married on Wednesday
Took ill on Thursday
Worse on Friday
Died on Saturday
Buried on Sunday
And that was the end of Solomon Grundy

5 Building words

A. If you know about prefixes and suffixes you can expand your vocabulary quickly and efficiently.

B. **Prefixes** are added to the **beginning of words**, often **adjectives**, to give them a **negative meaning**.

adjective	prefix	adjective
efficient	in-	inefficient
patient	im-	impatient
legal	il-	illegal
regular	ir-	irregular

C. The **prefixes 'dis-'** and **'un-'** can be added to **verbs**.

verb	prefix	verb
to agree	dis-	to disagree
to approve	dis-	to disapprove
to lock	un-	to unlock
to dress	un-	to undress

D. The **suffix '-er'** or **'-or'** is used for **tools** and for **people** who carry out **jobs**.

verb	suffix	noun
to write	-er	writer
to advise	-or	advisor
to open	-er	opener
to project	-or	projector

E. The **suffix '-(t)ion'** can be used to **make nouns** from **verbs**.

verb	suffix	noun
to produce	-tion	production
to pollute	-ion	pollution
to admire	-tion	admiration
to reduce	-tion	reduction

5 Practice

I. It's impossible to know exactly which prefix an adjective takes to make its opposite but these six are easy ones. Do you know them?

1.	possible	impossible	4.	happy	...
2.	secure	...	5.	relevant	...
3.	tolerant	...	6.	legible	...

II. Building new verbs is also quite easy because there are only two prefixes: 'un-' and 'dis-'. Complete the grid.

1.	to wrap	to unwrap	4.	to like	...
2.	to appear	...	5.	to plug	...
3.	to believe	...	6.	to please	...

III. What is it? It ends with the suffix '-er' or '-or'.

1. You play your CDs on it.
2. You cook your food with it.
3. A machine that grinds coffee.
4. A person who translates texts from one language into another.
5. A machine that washes dishes.
6. A man who acts in films or in the theatre.

IV. Look up the following words in your dictionary. They all have something to do with cars.

◆ windscreen wiper ◆ carburettor ◆ radiator ◆ speedometer

V. Complete these sentences. Use the noun from the verb in brackets.

1. There's a lot of ... in the software business. (compete)
2. We are very grateful for all the ... we received. (donate)
3. A worldwide ... in CO_2 will help the environment. (reduce)
4. There were some small ... during the operation. (complicate)
5. Do you know much about the student ... of the 1960s? (revolt)
6. The murder ... will take a number of weeks. (investigate)

6 Clothes

A. It is not easy to use the **word 'clothes'** correctly. Remember that …

- it is a **plural form** only: you **can't** say ~~'a clothes'~~ or ~~'two clothes'~~
- it is **one syllable**: 'clothes' /kləʊðz/
- if you want to talk about different things you wear (trousers, shirts etc) you can call them **'items of clothing'**

B. Some items of clothing are **plural words** only. Use **'some'** or **'a pair of'** but **not** 'a' or 'an'. Look at these sentences.

Where are my trousers?
These leggings are really uncomfortable.
I'd like to have some stripy pyjamas.
Do I need a pair of shorts?
She wants to buy two pairs of jeans.

C. You probably know most of these words already.

blouse	coat	dress
jacket	shirt	skirt
suit	socks	tie

D. But do you know these words? Read the definitions. Can you guess what the words mean in your first language?

belt:	a piece of leather which you wear around the waist
braces:	men wear them; they hold up their trousers
collar:	the part of the shirt around your neck
dinner jacket:	very formal clothes for men; worn in the evening
gloves:	you wear them on your hands when it's cold
heel:	part of the shoe, on the bottom and at the back
laces:	you tie your shoes up with them
sleeve:	part of a shirt (or jumper) that covers the arm
waistcoat:	you wear it over a shirt but under a jacket

6 Practice

I. Complete these sentences. Use one word only.

1. Do you need … new pair of jeans?
2. Where … my shorts? Have you seen them?
3. Why does she want to buy two … of leggings?
4. Look at this. It says that my pyjamas … made in Scotland.
5. These are my golfing trousers. What do you think of … ?
6. The difference between 'underpants' and 'knickers' is easy. Underpants … for men and knickers … for women!

II. Which words rhyme?

1. clothes	a. my
2. skirt	b. trousers
3. blouses	c. shoot
4. tie	d. hurt
5. suit	e. leave
6. sleeve	f. shows

III. Put the words in the box into the appropriate column.

blouse ◆ braces ◆ coat ◆ dress ◆ gloves ◆ jacket ◆ knickers ◆ shirt ◆ skirt ◆ socks ◆ tie ◆ underpants

men	women	men and women
⋮	⋮	⋮

IV. Link these groups of words.

1. hands	a. hat
2. arm	b. collar
3. head	c. feet
4. neck	d. trousers
5. legs	e. gloves
6. socks	f. sleeve

V. Look up this idiomatic expression in your dictionary.

Don't get your knickers in a twist!

7 Common mistakes

A. People who are learning English often have the same sort of difficulties. They find it hard to …

- use language which is appropriate
- select the correct language forms
- choose suitable vocabulary
- pronounce and stress words correctly

B. Using **appropriate language**. Here are some tips.

Use **'would'** and **'could'** in requests: *Could I borrow your dictionary?*
Use **question tags** to be less direct: *You're not from Canada, are you?*
Use **'please'** and **'thank you'**: *Can you help me, please? Oh, thank you.*

C. Selecting **correct forms**. Remember the **basics**.

Ask **questions** correctly: *Do you live here? Did you ring?*
Know the **irregular verb forms**: *They flew to San Francisco.*
Use **modal verbs** properly: *I'll see you next week.*

D. Choosing **suitable vocabulary**. Do you know these words?

wife ⇔ woman: *May I introduce you to my wife?*
bring ⇔ take: *We can take you to the station.*
check ⇔ control: *Can you check these figures?*

E. **Pronouncing** and **stressing words** properly. Try these!

❐ ❒ ❐
important

❒ ❐ ❐
impotent

❐ ❐ ❒
apple pie

❐ ❐ ❐ ❐ ❒
Marilyn Monroe

F. Understanding the **culture**. You can't generalise but think about …

- humour (especially irony)
- understatement
- politeness

7 Practice

I. Two of these sentences are orders. One is a request. Which is which?

1. Could you sit here, please.
2. Please sit here.
3. Sit here.

II. What makes these sentences very polite? Choose your answer from a, b, c.

a. *They all begin with 'I'.*
b. *The verbs are in the past tense.*
c. *They are all long sentences.*

1. I wanted to ask you if you could help me.
2. I was wondering if I could ask you a quick question.
3. I thought we might go out for a meal next week.
4. I was hoping you might agree.

III. Add a question tag.

1. We didn't see you in the post office yesterday, ...?
2. You haven't got a bike I could borrow by any chance, ...?
3. He's a vegetarian, ...?
4. They could come in our car, ...?
5. She used to live in France, ...?
6. I'm not fat, ... ?

IV. Say these sentences out loud. Are they in correct English?

1. We look forward to seeing you.
2. Would you be so kind as to sign your name here, please?
3. I feel like a cup of coffee.
4. I've got a dental appointment at ten o'clock tomorrow morning.

V. Do you find it funny?

◆ What's the difference between a crazy rabbit and a plastic £5 note?
◆ One's a mad bunny and the other's bad money!

◆ What has six legs, four ears and a tail?
◆ A man on a horse!

◆ What do you call a camel with three humps?
◆ Humphrey!

8 Containers and contents

A. The **word 'container'** is a **general** word. It refers to anything which you can use **to keep** or **transport** something in. There are many **different types** of containers.

a bottle	a can	a tin
a jar	a packet	a tube

B. A good way to learn these words is to learn their **contents**.

a bottle …	of wine	of lemonade
a can …	of Coca-Cola	of beer
a jar …	of jam	of (instant) coffee
a packet …	of biscuits	of cornflakes

C. Here are some more **containers** and what they **usually contain**.

a barrel …	of beer	of oil
a box …	of matches	of chocolates
a bowl …	of soup	of sugar
a bucket …	of water	of sand
a carton …	of yoghurt	of orange juice
a jug …	of water	of cream
a mug …	of tea	of coffee
a pack …	of cards	of cornflakes
a tin …	of beans	of fruit
a tube …	of toothpaste	of suncream

D. Often a **specific measure** is used instead of a container, particularly in recipes.

a pint …	of milk	a tablespoon …	of vinegar
half a pint …	of beer	two teaspoons …	of sugar
ten litres …	of petrol	fifty grams ...	of butter

E. Be careful with the meanings of some of these words on this page.

- a 'bowl' /bəʊl/ is a deep round dish for fruit, soup or sugar
- a 'carton' /ˈkɑːtən/ is a light plastic box for cream or yoghurt
- a 'glass' /glɑːs/ is not the same as a 'jar' /dʒɑː/. You say 'a glass of water' but 'a jar of jam' (or honey or coffee)

8 Practice

I. Complete the sentences. The words you need are all on page 20.

1. On the dining-room table there was a … of fruit.
2. They went to a sweet shop and bought a … of chocolates.
3. You buy instant coffee in …s.
4. The soup's ready! Can you put the …s on the table, please?
5. Many British people don't drink tea out of cups. They prefer …s.
6. Remember that in Britain you say a '…' of Coke but a '…' of beans.
7. Do we need another … of milk?
8. I've forgotten something! A … of chocolate biscuits!

II. These pairs of words are different in meaning. Give examples.

1. a pack - a packet
2. a glass - a jar
3. a box - a carton
4. a mug - a jug

III. Cross out two containers in each pair of brackets.

1. [a packet/a tin/a bucket] … of crisps
2. [a jar/a mug/ a sack] … of hot chocolate
3. [a barrel/a pack/a bottle] … of lemonade
4. [a bucket/a jug/a box] … of cream

IV. What material are these containers usually made of? Complete these sentences. (The first one has been done for you.)

1. A bottle is usually made of glass (or plastic).
2. A barrel …
3. A bucket …
4. A pack …
5. A tin …
6. A jar …

9 Correspondence

A. Each country has its own accepted way of writing a letter and laying it out. Here are some tips for writing letters to people in Britain.

B. Positioning the **address** and the **date**.

- the **writer's address** goes on the top right (but **not** the writer's name)
- the date is under the address

C. There are different **ways of beginning** a letter.

Dear Sir or Madam	**(formal and impersonal)**
Dear Mr/Mrs/Ms White	**(formal)**
Dear John/Joan	**(informal)**

Leave an empty line and start the first paragraph on the left with a **capital letter** (don't be afraid of starting with 'I')

23 Chestnut Lane
Swanston
Derbyshire
DE65 3TL

25 April 20..

Dear Mike

I got your letter yesterday ...

D. The **body of the letter** and the **end**.

- leave an empty line between paragraphs
- if you begin with *'Dear Sir or Madam'* end with *'Yours faithfully'*
- if you begin with *'Dear Mr/Mrs/Ms White'* end with *'Yours sincerely'*
- if you begin with *'Dear John/Joan'* end with *'Best wishes'* or *'With kind regards'*
- you can end with *'Love'* if it is someone close to you (but it is **not** usually used between men)

E. **Signing** your name and **afterthoughts**.

- sign with your **first name** and **family name** if it is a **formal** letter
- **don't** sign using your **title** (Mr/Mrs/Dr)
- sign with your **first name** if it is an **informal** letter
- you can add an **afterthought** after writing **PS** (Latin for 'post scriptum')

9 Practice

I. What are some of the differences between letters in Britain and letters in the country you come from?

II. Here are some parts of an informal letter. Put them in the correct order and lay them out on a piece of paper in the way described in sections B-E on the opposite page.

4 February 20..

Susan and Mark

We would leave on Friday and come back on Sunday and stay at a B&B somewhere. Give us a ring if you're interested and we can sort out the details.

Dear John and Joan

PS Did I leave my gloves at your place? I couldn't find them when I got back home.

43 Bridge Street
Royston
Buckinghamshire
HP16 9QP

Thanks once again. See you soon.

Love

Thanks very much for dinner yesterday. We really enjoyed it. Can Joan give us the recipe for the lasagne?

Mark and I are planning a weekend in Wales in March. Would you like to come with us?

10 Countries and regions

A. You probably know the names of most countries in Europe. Normally the **adjective** refers to the **language** and the **people** who live there, eg **Germany - German - a German**.

country	adjective	country	adjective
Austria	Austrian	Italy	Italian
Belgium	Belgian	Portugal	Portuguese
Denmark	Danish	Spain	Spanish
Finland	Finnish	Sweden	Swedish
France	French	Switzerland	Swiss

B. Be careful. **Some** nationalities have **special words** to refer to people.

She's a *Swede*. (*Swedish cars*)
He's a *Turk*. (*Turkish coffee*)
They're Spaniards. (*Spanish wine*)

C. Four countries make up the **United Kingdom** (often called **'Great Britain'** or **'Britain'**).

country	adjective
England	English
Wales	Welsh
Scotland	Scottish
Northern Ireland	Northern Irish

D. There are often English equivalents for **Länder** or **regions** in **German-speaking countries**. Here are some examples.

German	English
Hannover	Hanover
Hessen	Hesse
Kärnten	Carinthia
Niedersachsen	Lower Saxony
Oberfranken	Upper Franconia
Südtirol	South Tyrol

10 Practice

I. Complete this grid.

country	adjective	country	adjective
Argentina	...	Japan	...
...	Chinese	...	Korean
...	Greek	Mexico	...
...	Dutch	...	Norwegian
Israel	...	Turkey	...

II. Two words are missing from the front of this British passport. Which are they?

III. Complete this grid.

German	English
Wien	...
Nürnberg	...
...	Lake Constance
Köln	...
...	Danube
Schwarzwald	...

IV. Make sure you can say where you come from, which nationality you have and which languages you can speak.

11 Eating out

A. To get into a **popular restaurant** you have to **book a table** in advance.

- *Hello. I'd like to book a table.*
- *Yes, certainly. When for?*
- *For tomorrow if possible.*
- *Yes, of course. How many people?*
- *For four.*
- *Four. And what time?*
- *At eight o'clock if that's OK.*
- *Eight o'clock. Yes, that's fine. Could I just take your name, please?*
- *Yes, it's Parr. P - A - double R.*

B. Can you read the **menu**?

- Starter -
Asparagus soup

- Main course -
Roast beef and Yorkshire pudding

- Dessert -
Strawberries and cream

C. Sometimes there can be **problems**.

I'm sorry but …
- the meat's *tough*.
- the fish is *not cooked properly* (= *undercooked*).
- the vegetables are *overcooked*.
- the wine is *corked*.

I'd like to have something else, please.

D. **Paying** for the meal.

Could I have the bill, please?
VAT and service is included.
Of course you can pay by cheque if you wish.
We accept all major credit cards.
Shall I leave a tip for the waiter?

11 Practice

I. Put the following list of events (a-l) into a logical order (1-12). Start with line d and end with line l.

a. have the main course
b. ask for the bill
c. have the starter
d. book a table
e. go to the restaurant
f. order the food and drinks
g. leave a tip for the waiter
h. order the dessert
i. pay the bill
j. sit down
k. read the menu
l. leave the restaurant

II. Put the following into the correct column.

apple fritters ◆ chicken casserole ◆ chocolate mousse ◆ melon ◆ peach melba ◆ prawn cocktail ◆ roast duck ◆ tomato soup ◆ trout

starter	**main course**	**dessert**

III. Can you talk about typical food from the country - or region - you come from? These words and expressions may help you.

I don't know what you'd call it in English but …
It's difficult to describe but it's …
It's very similar to … .
It's something like …
It's very popular here and people eat it with …

12 Education and qualifications

A. It is not easy to talk about **education systems**. Each country has its own kind of schools - with their own special names - and often these vary from one region to another. In **Britain** children normally go to **three types of school**.

nursery school:	age 3-5
primary school:	age 5-10
secondary school:	age 11-16 and 16-18

B. It's common to **talk about** your **schooldays**.

to go to school
to be good at (subjects)
to take exams
to fail an exam
to repeat a year
to leave school at the age of …
to have lessons
to do tests
to pass an exam
to resit exams
to take school-leaving exams
to finish school at the age of …

C. Everybody has their favourite **school subjects**.

English	Maths	Biology	History	Music
German	Physics	Chemistry	Geography	Sport

D. Be careful with the verbs 'visit' and 'learn'.

He went to (not: ~~visited~~) *the local secondary school.*
She is revising (not: ~~learning~~) *for her exams.*

E. **After school** there are various possibilities.

to work for …	*(a person or a company)*
to train to become (not: ~~learn~~) …	*(a specific job or profession)*
to go to college to study …	*(a more practical course)*
to go to university to study …	*(a more academic course)*

F. For most **jobs** you need **qualifications**.

to get/have GCSEs (= General Certificate of Secondary Education) …
to get/have A (= Advanced) levels in …
to get/have a degree in …
to have a BA (= Bachelor of Arts) in …
to have a BSc (= Bachelor of Science) in …

12 Practice

I. Read this text.

'Where did I go to school? Well, I first went to a nursery school. I was only three so I can't remember it very well. Then, at the age of five, I went to the local primary school. I liked English and Sport but I wasn't very good at Maths. When I was ten I went to a secondary school. It was quite hard and I didn't do very well at the beginning. The teachers were quite strict and I was a bit lazy. However, it got easier when I could choose the subjects I wanted. I left school at sixteen and went to college to do business studies. When I was eighteen I got a job in an insurance company. In fact I still work there today.'

II. Now write a short text about your own education.

III. One of these sentences sounds wrong. Which one is it and why?

1. I learned for my exams and passed them all.
2. I passed my A levels and went to university to study Chemistry.
3. After college I worked for my father. He's got his own business.

IV. Join the beginnings and ends of the sentences.

1. After school I went to college ...	a. an American wine company.
2. When I was 18 ...	b. to study Electrical Engineering.
3. I worked for Gallo, ...	c. and got a diploma in Tourism.
4. I went to university ...	d. I trained to become a nurse.

V. Remember that the US school system is different from the British system. Test yourself by matching the left-hand column with the right-hand column.

1. quiz	a. pupil in 10th form
2. grades	b. marks
3. freshman	c. pupil in 9th form
4. sophomore	d. pupil in 11th form
5. junior	e. a short test

13 Electrical goods and tools

A. There are a lot of **electrical goods** around the **house**. You probably know these.

alarm clock	answerphone	camcorder	coffee grinder
cooker	dishwasher	food processor	freezer
fridge	hairdryer	hi-fi	hoover
iron	kettle	microwave	oven
television	toaster	video recorder	washing machine

B. Most people have **tools** at home, too. Here are some.

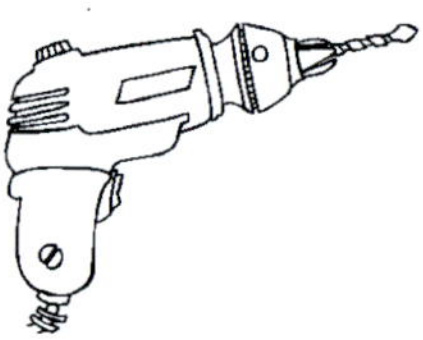
drill

hammer

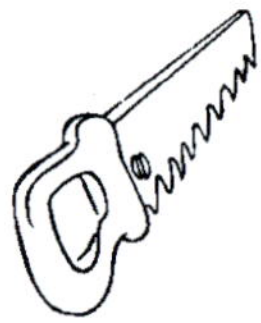
saw

pliers

raw plug

sandpaper

nail

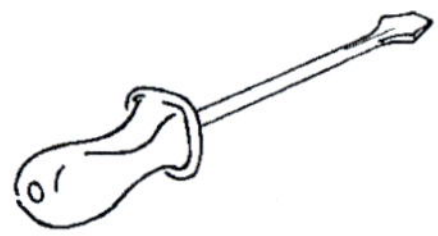
screwdriver

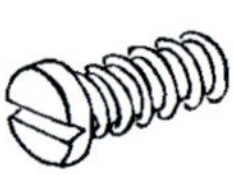
screw

spanner

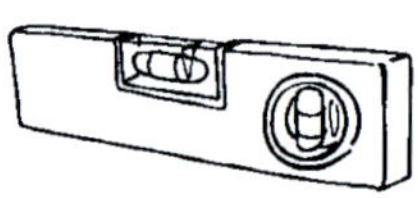
spirit level

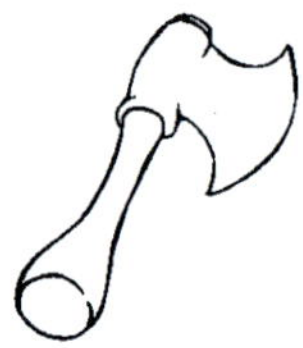
axe

C. The words **'electric'** and **'electrical'** are used differently.

- 'electric' is used with machines that are powered by electricity, eg 'an electric blanket', 'an electric fire', 'an electric guitar'
- 'electrical' is used before more general words, eg 'an electrical engineer', 'electrical appliances', 'electrical equipment'

13 Practice

I. Which of these electrical appliances are normally used in the kitchen, which in the bathroom and which in the lounge?

cooker ◆ dishwasher ◆ electric razor ◆ video recorder ◆ hi-fi ◆ hairdryer ◆ freezer ◆ television ◆ electric toothbrush

kitchen	bathroom	lounge

II. Say what you use it for. (The first sentence has been done for you.)

1. You use an answerphone for recording messages.
2. You use a kettle ... .
3. You use a hoover ... .
4. You use a microwave ... .
5. You use a fridge ... .
6. You use a hi-fi ... .

III. Which verb is missing from the sentences? Choose from the box.

change ◆ empty ◆ recharge ◆ set ◆ switch off ◆ touch

1. Have you ... the alarm clock? For seven o'clock?
2. Don't worry. I'll ... the TV when I go to bed.
3. I think we need to ... the bag in the hoover.
4. There are no more cups because I forgot to ... the dishwasher.
5. Don't ... the iron. It's very hot!
6. We can't film you at the moment because we need to ... the battery first.

IV. Which tools do you need? Complete the sentences. Use the words in section B.

1. To hang up a picture I need a ... and a ... .
2. To chop wood I need an ... .
3. To cut a piece of wood I need a ... .
4. To take the wheel off my bike I use a ... .
5. To take a raw plug out of the wall I use some ... .
6. To smooth a piece of wood I use ... .

14 Englishes

A. There are many words in **American English (AE)** which are **different** in **British English (BE)**.

AE	BE	German
fall	autumn	*Herbst*
cookies	biscuits	*Kekse*

B. Here are some **American English** words to do with **cars** and **travelling**.

AE	BE	AE	BE
gas	petrol	trunk	boot
truck	lorry	hood	bonnet
sidewalk	pavement	antenna	aerial

C. Some words in American English and British English **are the same** but **have different meanings**.

When they say the word:	an American person means:	which in German is:	but a British person means:	which in German is:
bill	paper money	*Geldschein*	a piece of paper telling you what you have paid	*Rechnung*
subway	an underground railway	*U-Bahn*	a tunnel under a busy road or railway line	*Unterführung*
mad	very angry	*wütend*	behaving unusually	*verrückt*
vest	sth you wear over your shirt	*Weste*	sth you wear under your shirt	*Unterhemd*
first floor	ground floor	*Erdgeschoss*	first floor	*1. Stock*
potato chips	sth cold and bought in different flavours	*Chips*	sth cooked in oil and eaten with ketchup	*Pommes Frites*

D. American English **spelling** is also different from British English spelling.

color (AE) - colour (BE) • center (AE) - centre (BE) • pajamas (AE) - pyjamas (BE) • TV program (AE) - TV programme (BE)

14 Practice

I. Complete the grid.

AE	BE	AE	BE
...	holiday	gas	...
elevator	...	...	biscuits
...	pavement	fall	...

II. Write these words using AE spelling.

AE	BE	AE	BE
...	to practise	...	litre
...	tyre	...	defence
...	humour	...	cheque

III. An American friend of yours is visiting you. Would you always understand what he or she says? Try this quiz.

1. Your American friend says he wants to have 'bills'? Where is he when he says this?
a) in a bank b) in a restaurant c) in a police car

2. Your American friend would like some 'chips'. What does he want?
a) something warm b) something cold c) something frozen

3. You're standing outside the house where you live. You say your apartment is on the 'second floor'. Does your American guest expect to walk up …
a) one flight of stairs? b) two flights of stairs? c) three flights of stairs?

4. Your American friend says he's taking the 'subway'. What does he mean?
a) he's going by bus b) he's going on foot c) he's going by train

5. Your American friend would like to buy a 'vest'. Does he mean an item of clothing that people …
a) can see? b) can't see? c) mustn't see?

15 False friends

A. What are 'false friends'?

They are words in **German** and **English** which **look the same** but **have different meanings**. Here are some examples you probably already know.

English		German
chef	≠	*Chef*
mustn't	≠	*muss nicht*
meaning	≠	*Meinung*
eventually	≠	*eventuell*

B. Here are some more false friends. Don't trust them!

German	←← English	German →→	English
praktisch	handy	*Handy*	mobile (phone)
eigentlich	actually	*aktuell*	current
werden	become	*bekommen*	get
Hausschuh	slipper	*Slipper*	slip-on shoe

C. 'No friends' are English words or expressions you hear but which **do not exist** in English.

You hear ...	but what people mean is ...
oldtimer	vintage car
twen	somebody in their twenties
pullunder	sleeveless jumper
dressman	male model
smoking	dinner jacket (BE), tuxedo (AE)
mobbing	hostility and antagonism at work
playback	miming (to pre-recorded music)

D. Be careful with these expressions. They are 'close friends'!

You hear ...	but what you should say is ...
last not least	last but not least
a happy end	a happy ending

15 Practice

I. Cross out the wrong word in each pair of brackets.

1. I've got a really nice [chef/boss]. She trusts me to do my work properly.
2. You [mustn't/needn't] touch the fence! It's electrified!
3. You know what I think about speed limit on motorways. What's your [meaning/opinion]?
4. We walked for miles and miles and [perhaps/eventually] we came to a pub.

II. Which word from section B is missing in these sentences? Use it in its correct form.

1. I find a laptop very ... because it means I can work on the train.
2. He doesn't like getting up early. Well, he hates it ...!
3. We're ... a new car next week. You must come and see it.
4. I used to have ... but I prefer ones with laces now.

III. Complete this grid by adding the English words.

	German	←← English	German →→	English
1.	*ausgeben*	spend	*spenden*	...
2.	*Leichenbestatter*	undertaker	*Unternehmer*	...
3.	*Koch*	chef	*Chef*	...
4.	*Kritiker/in*	critic	*Kritik*	...
5.	*Geschenk*	gift	*Gift*	...
6.	*mitfühlend*	sympathetic	*sympathisch*	...

IV. Now complete this grid by adding the German words.

	German	←← English	German →→	English
1.	...	gymnasium	*Gymnasium*	a type of secondary school
2.	...	ordinary	*ordinär*	vulgar
3.	...	pass	*Pass*	a passport
4.	...	promotion	*Promotion*	a doctoral degree
5.	...	buckle	*Buckel*	a hump
6.	...	to probe	*proben*	to rehearse

16 Family and friends

A. You probably know these words.

mother	daughter	sister	aunt	nephew	grandfather
father	son	brother	uncle	grandmother	grandchildren

B. But do you know these words?

niece: your brother's or sister's daughter
sister-in-law: your brother's wife
stepfather: your mother's husband (but not your father)

C. Not everybody is your friend.

somebody I met recently: somebody you met by chance and hardly know
an acquaintance: somebody you know - but not very well
a close friend: a very good friend
a mate: an informal word for a good friend (eg classmate)

D. Remember that in English …

- the word 'boyfriend' usually means a girl's or woman's close male friend (but not a boy's or man's close male friend)
- the word 'girlfriend' usually means a boy's or man's close friend (but a girl or woman can also use this word)
- the correct English expression is 'a friend of mine' (**not** 'a friend of ~~me~~')

E. People often talk about their **relationships with others**.

Mike can't stand his boss.
Steve and Liz get on well.
Jackie's fallen out with her parents.
Dave and Susan have broken up.
Tom and Clare had a terrible argument but I think they've made up.

F. There are also many **idiomatic expressions** which describe how well people get on with each other.

They don't see eye to eye.
They get on like a house on fire.
They just can't hit it off.

16 Practice

I. Put these words into the correct category.

aunt ◆ brother ◆ daughter ◆ father ◆ grandfather ◆ grandmother ◆ niece ◆ mother ◆ nephew ◆ sister ◆ son ◆ uncle

male	female
nephew	niece

II. Look at this family tree. Complete the sentences about Alan.

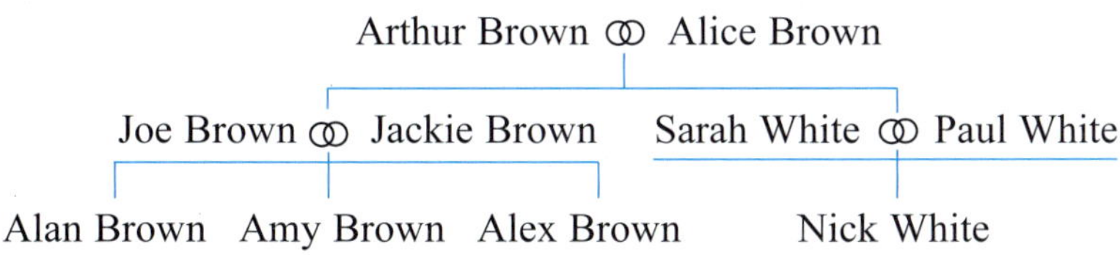

1. Amy is Alan's … .
2. Alex is Alan's … .
3. Joe is Alan's … .
4. Jackie is Alan's … .
5. Arthur is Alan's … .
6. Alice is Alan's … .
7. Sarah is Alan's … .
8. Paul is Alan's … .

III. Put the words in the box into the correct sentences.

broken up ◆ can't stand ◆ fallen out ◆ hit it off ◆ made up

1. Rebecca … her boss so she's looking for another job.
2. Kevin has … with his parents and is moving into his own flat.
3. After being together for three years Terry and Rachel have … .
4. Roger and Amy had an awful argument but they've … now.
5. Poor Lucy! Her parents can't … with her new boyfriend!

IV. Remember this rhyme.

Let's share the air!

17 Food and drink

A. You can **categorise food** and **words to do with food** in different ways.

fruit:	apple, pear, grape, pineapple
meat:	chicken, pork, lamb, beef
vegetables:	potatoes, beans, spinach, carrots
ways of cooking:	baking, frying, boiling, grilling

B. There are many more everyday words and expressions you may need when you're sitting at the table.

Could you pass the salt, please?
Shall I get you another spoon?
Would you like some mustard?
Excuse me. Have you got any black pepper?

C. If you're eating, you're probably **drinking**.

beer:	lager, bitter
soft drinks:	lemonade, orange juice
spirits:	whisky, gin, brandy
wine:	white, red, rosé

D. **Herbs** and **spices** are popular. Do you know these words?

herbs:	parsley, rosemary, chives
spices:	cinnamon, ginger, nutmeg

E. Be careful with the **pronunciation** of these words.

onion	/ˈʌnjən/
lettuce	/ˈletɪs/
pizza	/ˈpiːtsə/
sausages	/ˈsɒsɪdʒəz/
raspberry	/ˈrɑːzbərɪ/
apple pie	/ˌæpəl ˈpaɪ/

17 Practice

I. Put the words in the box into the correct category.

apricot ◆ asparagus ◆ cauliflower ◆ celery ◆ melon ◆ courgette ◆ lemon ◆ leek ◆ orange ◆ strawberry

fruit	vegetable

II. Six types of meat. Can you name the other three?

from a pig:	...	...	bacon
from a sheep:	...	mutton	
from a calf:	veal		

III. Is it the same? If not, say why.

1. a 'pint of lager' and 'a pint of bitter'
2. 'apple juice' and 'cider'
3. a 'large brandy' and a 'double brandy'
4. an 'old wine' and a 'vintage wine'

IV. Complete these well-known pairs. You need one word.

1. salt and …
2. knife and …
3. milk and …
4. gin and …
5. fish and …
6. bread and ...

V. Practise your pronunciation.

salmon: /ˈsæmən/ a pink fish
claret: /ˈklærət/ a red wine from Bordeaux
thyme: /taɪm/ a type of herb

VI. Get it?

➢ What did the tomato say to the cucumber?
➢ Lettuce get married!

18 Greetings and small talk

A. Greeting people you **don't know**.

Formal greeting used when you first meet somebody	
How do you do.	(✋ shake hands)
Pleased to meet you.	(✋ shake hands)

People in Britain only shake hands when they meet somebody for the first time or when they haven't seen each other for a long time.

B. Greeting people you **do know**.

More informal greeting used when you know somebody	
Hello (there).	(don't shake hands)
Hi (there).	(don't shake hands)

C. Asking about somebody's **health** - and **replying**.

How are you? - *Fine, thanks.*
How are you doing? - *Very well, thanks.*
How you doing? - *Oh, not too bad.*
How're things? - *OK.*
How're things going? - *Can't complain.*

D. People often **comment on the weather**.

Glorious weather, isn't it?
Mmm! It's lovely outside!
What awful weather!
It's a bit chilly out there.
It's a beautiful day today!
What a terrible day!
It's really miserable today.
Wrap up warm! It's freezing!

(Remember you can't say ~~a weather~~!)

E. It's polite **to offer** somebody **something**.

Would you like something to drink?
Can I get you something to eat?
Shall I put the kettle on?
Cup of coffee? Milk? Sugar?
I'm just going to have a cup of tea? Would you like one?

18 Practice

I. Find a suitable reply (a-h).

1. How are you?
2. How do you do.
3. What's the weather like?
4. Can I get you something?
5. How's your brother?
6. Milk and sugar?
7. Hi there!
8. What a lovely day.

a. It's awful. Cold and raining.
b. Oh, hello? What are you doing here?
c. Just milk, please. Lovely.
d. Yes, it's beautiful.
e. How do you do.
f. Fine, thanks.
g. Oh, yes. A cup of tea, please.
h. He's OK. Very busy at the moment.

II. Complete the sentences. Use the correct expression from the box.

feels that you have disturbed them ◆ is disappointed ◆ wins a prize ◆ says 'thank you' ◆ sneezes loudly ◆ talks too quietly ◆ would like to go through a door in front of you ◆ wants to use your phone to make a quick call

1. When somebody … you say 'Bless you!'
2. When somebody … you say 'Congratulations!'
3. When somebody … you say 'After you!'
4. When somebody … you say 'Nevermind!'
5. When somebody … you say 'I'm so sorry!'
6. When somebody … you say 'Pardon?'
7. When somebody … you say 'Of course. Go ahead.'
8. When somebody … you say 'You're welcome.'

III. Put these sentences into the correct order to make an eight-line dialogue. Start with line e.

a. Cup of coffee?
b. Great! Come in.
c. Hi. I was in the area so I thought I'd see if you were in.
d. Is it? I haven't been out today. Sugar?
e. John! Hi! What are you doing here?
f. No, thanks. Just milk.
g. Oh, that'd be lovely. It's a bit chilly outside.
h. Thanks. I won't stay long.

19 Health and fitness

A. What's the problem?

I've got a terrible cough.	*I feel tired.*	*My arm hurts.*
I've got stomach ache.	*I feel dizzy.*	*My leg is sore.*
I've got toothache.	*I feel sick.*	*My back aches.*
I've got a headache.	*I feel faint.*	*My eyes are red.*
I've got a sore throat.	*I feel weak.*	*My knee is stiff.*
I've got a temperature.	*I feel funny.*	*My feet are always cold.*
I've got a pain in my chest.	*I feel hot.*	*My ankle is swollen.*

B. And is there anything else?

Yes, I can't
- *stop coughing.*
- *sleep properly.*
- *bend my elbow.*
- *climb stairs without having to stop.*

C. Mmm. Well, I'm not quite sure but ...

I think
- *you've got the flu.*
- *you've got pneumonia.*
- *you've got arthritis.*
- *you've got a problem with your thyroid.*
- *you've sprained your ankle.*
- *you need to see a specialist.*
- *- to be quite honest - you're wasting my time!*

D. Do you look after yourself?

I do sport regularly - three times a week.
I'm very careful about what I eat - lots of fresh fruit and vegetables.
I don't smoke - not even a pipe.
I drink - but only in moderation.

E. What else?

I'm allergic to cats.
I'm short-sighted. I wear contact lenses.
My new shoes have given me blisters.
No, of course I'm not a hypochondriac! Ouch! My foot hurts!

19 Practice

I. What is it? Link the numbers with the letters.

1. arthritis	a. a swelling on the edge of the eyelid
2. a stroke	b. when you are hit hard in the eye and it goes dark blue
3. a rash	c. an attack in the brain
4. a sty	d. an area of red spots on the skin
5. a black eye	e. very painful stiffness on the muscles and joints

II. Match the beginnings and ends of the sentences.

1. If you're constipated	a. you want to scratch it.
2. If you're pregnant	b. you need an operation.
3. If you've broken your leg	c. you're going to have a baby.
4. If your skin itches	d. you get sunburn.
5. If you smoke a lot	e. there's not much you can do about it.
6. If you get the flu	f. you can't go to the toilet.
7. If you've got appendicitis	g. it is put in plaster.
8. If you stay too long in the sun	h. it is bad for your health.

III. Which of the following are good for your health? Can you add some of your own ideas?

- Drinking lots of water ❐
- Getting a good night's sleep ❐
- Eating chips and ketchup ❐
- Drinking beer every day ❐
- Getting plenty of exercise ❐

IV. Can you pronounce these words correctly?

1. pneumonia	/njuːˈməʊnɪə/	3. bruise	/bruːz/
2. diarrhoea	/ˌdaɪəˈrɪə/	4. arthritis	/ɑːˈθraɪtɪs/

V. Doctor, doctor!

➢ Doctor, Doctor! Everybody keeps ignoring me!
Next, please.

➢ Doctor, Doctor! I've swallowed a film!
Nevermind. Let's see how it develops.

20 Hobbies and games

A. You will already know the names of many **freetime activities**.

doing sport	gardening
going for a drink with friends	going to the cinema/theatre
listening to music	photography
playing chess/cards	playing the guitar
reading	stamp collecting

B. **Hobbies** are activities which are **not competitive**. Link the following activities to their definitions.

1. knitting	a. dropping from an aeroplane
2. rambling	b. collecting the numbers of railway engines
3. parachuting	c. joining wool together to make clothes
4. train spotting	d. walking in the countryside

C. There are many different **types of sports** but some are more popular than others. Check you know these.

basketball	cycling
football	golf
gymnastics	hang-gliding
inline skating	jogging
skiing	swimming
walking	windsurfing

D. Saying what you **like** - and **don't like**.

I like ...	*I enjoy ...*
I'm interested in ...	*I don't mind ... but I prefer ...*
I get a lot of pleasure from ...	*I'm not so fond of ...*
I'm keen on ...	*I'm not a great fan of ...*

20 Practice

I. Alone or two of you? Which of these activities go into which column?

going for a drink with friends ◆ having flying lessons ◆ listening to music ◆ photography ◆ playing an instrument ◆ playing chess ◆ parachuting ◆ reading ◆ stamp collecting ◆ water skiing

you can do it alone	you must do it with another person

II. What are these people talking about? The answers are in section C.

1. 'No, I don't really like it. It's too slow. You have to walk from one hole to another and then wait. It's very difficult, too. I've been playing for three years and I don't think I've improved at all.'

2. 'It's OK when the water's warm and there are not many people in the pool. But I don't like it in the winter when you've got to get changed. It's too much trouble.'

3. 'I love it. It's lovely to get up on a sunny morning and go for a ride. You don't need a car, you don't need any special equipment. You just go. It's good for your health and it's good for the environment!'

III. For what game do you need these words?

1. heart - club - diamond - spade

2. bishop - king - pawn - knight

3. hotel - house - jail - free parking

4. birdie - par - green - tee

IV. Write a short text (50 - 80 words) saying what you like to do - or don't like to do - in your freetime. Use some of the expressions in section D.

21 Holidays

A. Where people **spend their holidays**.

bed and breakfast
guest house
hotel
time-share apartment
camp site
holiday camp
self-catering accommodation
youth hostel

B. Asking about a room.

- *Good afternoon. Can I help you?*
- *Yes, I wanted to know if you've got any rooms available?*
- *Yes. One moment. A double?*
- *No, a single.*
- *A single. Just for one night?*
- *No, two.*
- *OK. That's fine. Would you like a bath or a shower?*
- *A bath, please.*
- *That's £70 per night including breakfast.*
- *OK. I'll take it. Can I pay by credit card?*
- *Yes, of course.*
- *Good.*
- *Perhaps you could fill in this form and I'll get someone to take your bags.*

C. What people **do on holiday**.

eating out
go sightseeing
go walking
hire a car and travel around
lie on the beach
read a good book
relax and do nothing special
swim in the sea

D. What people expect **hotels to offer**.

a sea view
air conditioning
conference facilities
full board
half board
evening entertainment
indoor pool
mini-bar
sauna
underground parking

21 Practice

I. Which word from section A is it?

1. a flat or house where you do your own cooking
2. a small, simple place where you spend the night and get breakfast
3. a flat you can go to at certain times of the year
4. a large house with cheap rooms where young people stay

II. Which activities are these people describing? Some of them are in section C.

1. 'I don't mind the heat. And I don't mind the people. I usually have a book or a newspaper and read. For me it's not a proper holiday if I come back and I'm not brown.'

2. 'I like the smell best. Oh, yes, and I like the waves, too. I don't mind if the water's cold.'

3. 'Why do you have to do something on holiday? I have enough to do at home.'

4. 'I want to learn more about the country where I'm staying. I want to find out about its history, its people and its customs.'

III. Read this extract from a holiday brochure. Is this a description of a youth hostel, a guest house or a hotel?

Welcome to our home

'It's not just near the sea, it's on the sea'

David and Chris Grant would like to welcome you to Corisande Manor, a mansion built for an Austrian count in Victorian times. It has a host of interesting original features, like the ceiling made from the timbers of a 300-year-old Spanish schooner that sunk in the bay. Corisande is set right on the sea in Cornwall. The Manor and sheltered grounds face south and have wonderful views over the sea and sands below. It is a small personally run establishment with only 19 bedrooms.

Corisande is quietly set in 3 acres of grounds and fronts directly onto the sea, with private access to the Gannel sands. You can walk for miles along the beaches or relax in our garden. You can explore all of Cornwall by car (we are very central and most places are within 40 minutes' drive), or swim on numerous sandy beaches. In short, you can be as energetic or lethargic as you please.

22 Houses and homes

A. A network can help you to remember words connected with houses.

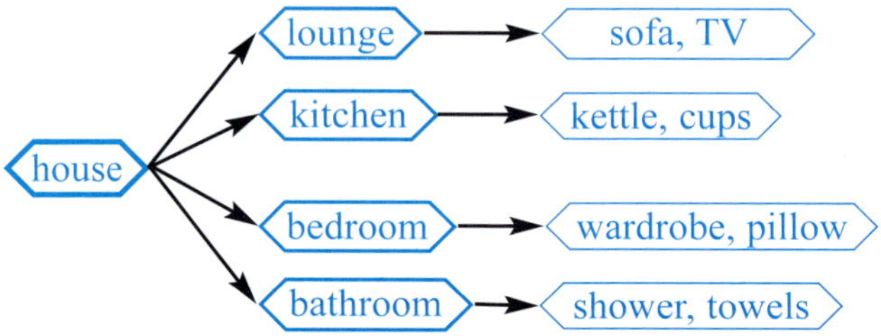

B. These are all **parts of a house**. Do you know what they are?

1. A conservatory		an area at the top of the stairs.
2. A dining room		an area you first come into in a house.
3. A hall	is	a room with glass walls and a glass roof.
4. A landing		a room where you work.
5. A study		a room where meals are eaten.

C. Rooms contain **items of furniture**.

armchair	bookshelf
chest of drawers	cupboard
desk	settee
stool	wardrobe

D. These words are often used when talking about houses and rooms. Read the definitions.

bunk beds:	two beds on top of each other
double glazing:	windows with two panes of glass
gas-fired central heating:	central heating powered by gas
lawn:	area of grass in front of and behind a house
pantry:	small room where you can keep food
porch:	covered area around the front door
shed:	wooden hut for garden tools
utility room:	small room for washing machine, freezer

22 Practice

I. In which room would you probably find these things? Put them into the correct column. Which three items would you find in all four rooms?

CDs ◆ computer ◆ cutlery ◆ dishwasher ◆ encyclopaedia ◆ envelopes ◆ floor and ceiling ◆ light switch ◆ razor ◆ settee ◆ tin opener ◆ power point ◆ toothbrush ◆ towel ◆ video recorder

kitchen	lounge	study	bathroom	all rooms

II. In which part of the house would you do these things? Choose a word from section B.

1. have dinner with eight friends
2. sit and read the paper on a sunny afternoon in February
3. write a long letter to your bank manager
4. say: 'Hello! Come in! Can I take your coat?'

III. What's the difference between ...

1. a 'chair' and an 'armchair'?
2. a 'wardrobe' and a 'chest of drawers'?
3. a 'desk' and a 'table'?
4. a 'hall' and a 'landing'?

IV. Choose words from section D to complete these sentences.

1. If you want to have more space in a bedroom you can buy … .
2. A … is useful if you've got lots of garden tools.
3. … is expensive but it makes your house warm and reduces heating costs.
4. British people like gardening and making their …s look good.

V. Look up these words in your dictionary.

1. a detached house
2. a semi-detached house
3. a terraced house

23 Idioms

A. What is an idiom?

An **idiom** is a **fixed expression**. Its meaning is not usually clear from the individual words. Look at this example. *'Sally's over the moon. She's passed her driving test!'* The expression *to be over the moon* has nothing to do with the moon. It means *to be very happy*.

B. Be careful when using idioms.

People like to use idioms because they are personal, informal and often humorous. Learners of English, however, should be careful **to use** them **appropriately**. If you are not sure what an idiom means or if it can be used in a certain situation (or in front of a certain person), don't use it!

C. Look at these idiomatic expressions and what they mean.

I'm keeping a low profile.	(I'm making sure nobody notices me)
It was a piece of cake.	(It was easy)
Keep your fingers crossed!	(Wish me good luck)
Keep your hair on!	(Don't get excited - stay calm)
She let the cat out of the bag.	(She told a secret)

D. Here are some more idioms.

1. *We don't really like him. He thinks he's the bee's knees.*
   (= better than anybody else)
2. *I've got that stupid song on the brain.*
   (= not able to stop thinking about it)
3. *It doesn't work. We'll have to go back to square one.*
   (= start from the beginning)
4. *When it comes to maths, she's really on the ball.*
   (= to know a lot)

23 Practice

I. These idioms all have something to do with how people feel. Are they positive feelings or negative?

He's on cloud nine.
She's over the moon.

II. These idioms describe people's health. Their meanings should be clear. Cross out the word you don't need.

He's a bit under the weather.	(He's feeling well/a bit sick.)
She's as fit as a fiddle.	(She's ill/very well indeed.)

III. These are connected with communication problems. Complete the second sentence.

I can't get a word in edgeways.	(The other person is … all the time!)
They're always talking shop!	(They are always talking about their … !)

IV. These idioms describe parts of the day. Circle the correct meaning.

I'm going to put my feet up.	(play chess - relax - do acrobatics)
I'm ready to crash out now.	(have a drink - go to a disco - go to bed)

V. These idioms appeared in the Fast Track books. Link them to their correct explanations.

1. to have forty winks
2. to pay an arm and a leg for sth
3. to spend a penny
4. to turn a blind eye to sth

a. to praise sb
b. to ignore sth
c. to pay by cheque for sth
d. to have a short sleep
e. to go to the toilet
f. to pay a lot for sth

24 Insurance

A. Read this short text about insurance.

'Insurance is a pooling of risks. This means that the money paid by each person or company, the premium, goes into a pool. This pool is then invested and used to pay out when a misfortune occurs to a person or company and they feel the need to make a claim. That is, they call on their insurance company to pay out compensation for the loss they've suffered. Your insurance policy is a contract with your insurance company.'

B. Here are two more important words from the world of insurance.

liable: responsible by law for something that has happened
negligent: when you did not do something which you were supposed to do

C. Read about liability.

- Public liability: If a shop owner has just washed the floor and a customer slips and breaks a leg then the shop owner is liable. He is obliged to pay financial compensation.
- Products liability: If a manufacturer's products cause illness or injury to a customer then the manufacturer is liable and must pay compensation to the injured party.

D. Look at these words which are often used in connection with **motor insurance.**

- a no-claims discount
  money you save on your premium because you haven't made an insurance claim
- voluntary excess
  the amount of money you pay when you make a claim
- fully-comprehensive insurance
  insurance which covers damage to your car and someone else's car
- third-party fire and theft insurance
  insurance which only covers damage to someone else's car
- a cover note
  a temporary document
- a policy
  a contract with your insurance company giving all the details of your cover

24 Practice

Test yourself. Choose the best alternative to complete each sentence.

1. Insurance companies can be considered as professional ... takers.
   a) life b) risk c) chance d) misfortune

2. Some of the language in insurance ... is incomprehensible to most ordinary people.
   a) premiums b) policies c) rates d) invoices

3. Insurance companies like you to ... your claim as soon as possible.
   a) process b) submit c) assure d) proceed

4. Go to an insurance ... and see if you can get a better deal.
   a) breaker b) broker c) speculator d) merchant

5. In times like these it is important to keep the value of your policy closely ... to the value of your house.
   a) adapted b) linked c) indicated d) dependent

6. My insurance company offers a wide ... of cover.
   a) range b) branch c) rank d) standard

7. His insurance company had told her not to admit ..., even though it was obviously her fault.
   a) legality b) likelihood c) liability d) crime

8. My life assurance policy will ... when I'm sixty-five.
   a) ripen b) mature c) flourish d) break

9. ... insurance has its origins in the fifteenth century.
   a) Boat b) Sea c) Navy d) Marine

10. The insurance will be ... if you omit any relevant information.
    a) void b) valid c) invaluable d) useless

11. Make sure all this equipment is insured ... accidental damage.
    a) over b) against c) with d) from

12. If you cause illness or injury to a customer and you are liable then you are obliged to pay compensation ... the injured party.
    a) for b) with c) to d) on

25 Jobs and work

A. There are various ways of **asking about** somebody's job.

What do you do?
What do you do for a living?
What's your line of business?

B. In Britain **job titles** are probably not used as much as in other countries. Instead people **prefer to describe** where they work or what their job is.

I work for a company that makes tyres.
I'm in the export division at TWB.
I'm responsible for dealing with the correspondence.

C. It is impossible to list all the **jobs people do**. Here are some.

skilled manual work	professions
butcher	dentist
chef	doctor
dressmaker	architect
electrician	vet
hairdresser	lawyer
mechanic	engineer
plumber	accountant

D. People like to **talk about** their jobs.

to be without a job
to apply for a job
to be offered a job
to start a new job
to work freelance
to have flexitime
to take early retirement
to be given a pay rise
to change one's job
to be invited for an interview
to accept a job offer
to work regular hours
to work shifts
to be on maternity leave
to be promoted
to be made redundant

25 Practice

I. Make sure you distinguish between these two questions. Translate them into your own language.

1. What are you doing? - I'm waiting for my sister.
2. What do you do? - I'm an architect.

II. Which job is the odd one out? Can you say why?

1. nurse - secretary - police officer
2. mechanic - priest - plumber
3. carpenter - politician - chef
4. teacher - vet - farmer

III. Put these verbs in a logical sequence 1-9. Start with g.

a. to accept a job offer
b. to apply for a job
c. to be given a pay rise
d. to be invited for an interview
e. to be made redundant
f. to be offered a job
g. to be without a job
h. to start a new job
i. to work hard

IV. Read what this personnel manager says about recruiting staff into the retail business.

'We receive about eight thousand application forms in the UK and we receive about two thousand application forms in Europe. So we shortlist those forms and we draw up the lists of people that we want to interview.

The interviewer is looking for evidence of five key skills: leadership, planning and organising, assertiveness, analytical consideration and job motivation. But we're also looking for people whose real interest lies in retail, who really get motivated by - and get a buzz from - working in retail and working with the customer.'

26 Key verbs

A. The verbs **'be'**, **'do'** and **'have'** are important verbs in English because with them you can make **questions**, **negatives**, **short answers**, **continuous forms**, **perfect forms** and **passive forms**.

I'm listening.
Did you see me yesterday? No, I didn't.
Where were you going?
Have you been to Australia. Yes, I have.
Didn't you know I had an uncle in Sydney?
They were asked to come a bit later.

B. Another key verb in English is **'get'**. Look at these example sentences.

I got an e-mail from Kathy today.	(receive)
Can you get some butter from the supermarket?	(buy)
It's getting dark. Let's go inside.	(become)
We got to the hotel at ten o'clock in the evening.	(arrive)
Shall I get you a glass of water?	(fetch)

C. Look carefully at **'get'** in these sentences.

We got to the airport twenty minutes before the plane was due to leave.
We got home on Sunday evening.

D. The verb **'get'** has some **specific meanings**, too.

He told me a joke but I didn't get it.	(understand)
Her silly remarks really get me!	(annoy)

E. The verb **'get'** combines with **particles** (**'on'**, **'over'**, **'through'** etc) to form **multi-word verbs**.

Victoria is getting on well at school.	(progress)
Did you get through your maths exam?	(pass)
She's getting over a bad cold.	(recover from)
David got through all his pocket money in one day.	(use up)

26 Practice

I. Read the six questions. Which sentence contains 'be', which 'do' and which 'have' as primary auxiliaries? Write the numbers into the grid.

1. Did you want to speak to me?
2. Were you thinking of coming with us?
3. Was he invited to the party?
4. Have you been to India?
5. Do you know Jill very well?
6. Had the bus already left when they arrived?

be	do	have

II. Make these sentences sound informal by using 'get'.

1. We're all becoming older, aren't we?
2. We received a postcard from Don yesterday.
3. We arrived home in the middle of the night.
4. Can you buy some stamps for me on your way home?
5. Do you understand this question? I don't know what it means!
6. Could you fetch my wallet from the kitchen, please?

III. Match the multi-word verbs with 'get' and the explanations (a-f) in the box.

a. to avoid doing something you are supposed to do
b. to begin something you think is important
c. to communicate with somebody
d. to do something you probably shouldn't do
e. to survive on
f. to start a long journey

1. We can't <u>get by on</u> one salary.
2. It's very quiet. I wonder what the children are <u>getting up to</u>?
3. It's high time I <u>got down</u> to my homework.
4. I'm going to try and <u>get out of</u> my piano lesson tomorrow afternoon.
5. We packed the night before and <u>got off</u> early in the morning.
6. I keep telling him but I can't <u>get through to</u> him. He won't listen!

27 Legal matters

A. The verb **'to steal'** is quite common. It is usually used with **things**. Remember to use it correctly.

They stole a car.
I've had my car stolen.

B. The verb **'to rob'** is usually used with **places**. In **passive sentences** it often takes the **preposition 'of'**.

He robbed the bank.
She was robbed of all her belongings.

C. Look at some more **crimes** and how they are defined.

Crime	**What it is**
arson	to set fire to a building or house (on purpose)
assault	to attack somebody physically and violently
bribery	to give somebody money in return for help
burglary	to steal something from somebody's house
forgery	to make a copy of something to deceive somebody
manslaughter	to kill somebody (without intending to)
murder	to kill somebody (on purpose)
rape	to force somebody to have sex when they do not want to
shoplifting	to steal goods from a shop by leaving without paying
theft	a more formal word for stealing

D. Look at this **sequence of events**.

↓ *Somebody commits a crime.*
↓ *They are accused of a crime.*
↓ *They are taken to court.*
↓ *The trial begins.*
↓ *The evidence is heard.*
↓ *The verdict is passed.*
↓ *The defendant is acquitted* (= to say somebody is not guilty).
↓ *The defendant is found guilty.*

27 Practice

I. Match the verbs (1-15) with the expressions on the right (a-o).

1. to accuse someone	a. in cold blood
2. to arrest someone	b. to court
3. to ban	c. the law
4. to break	d. a telephone box
5. to charge someone	e. for armed robbery
6. to commit	f. a witness
7. to cross-examine	g. a passport
8. to forge	h. with murder
9. to hijack	i. smoking in public places
10. to murder someone	j. of shoplifting
11. to pinch	k. £500
12. to rob	l. a terrible crime
13. to steal	m. a bar of chocolate
14. to take someone	n. an aeroplane
15. to vandalize	o. a bank

II. Read these three texts. Which crimes did these people commit?

fraud ◆ murder ◆ shoplifting ◆ manslaughter ◆ assault

In 1981 Marianne Bachmeier was in court watching the trial of Klaus Grabowski, who had murdered her 7-year-old daughter. During the trial Frau Bachmeier pulled a pistol from her handbag and fired eight bullets, six of which hit Grabowski, killing him. The defence said she had bought the weapon with the intention of committing suicide but when she saw Grabowski she drew the pistol and pulled the trigger. She was given six years' imprisonment. ______

***

In 1952 two youths in Mitcham, London decided to rob a dairy. They were Christopher Craig, aged 16 and Derek Bentley, 19. During the robbery they were disturbed by a policeman. Craig produced a gun and killed him. At the time Britain still had the death penalty. As Craig was under eighteen he was sentenced to life imprisonment. Bentley, although he never touched the gun, was hanged. Capital punishment was abandoned in 1965. ______

***

In June 1980 Lady Isobel Barnet was convicted of stealing a tin of tuna fish and a carton of cream, total value 87p, from a small shop. She was fined £75 and was ordered to pay £200 towards the cost of the case.

28 Letters

A. It is important to be able to understand and say the **letters of the alphabet** in English. One way of remembering the sound of the letters is by organising them into groups.

eɪ	iː	e	ɑɪ	əʊ	juː	ɑː
a	b	f	i	o	q	r
h	c	l	y		u	
j	d	m			w	
k	e	n				
	g	s				
	p	x				
	t	z				
	v					

B. As soon as letters are put in words they are pronounced differently. In fact **some letters** are **not pronounced** at all.

high /haɪ/
spaghetti /spəˈgetɪ/
car /kɑː/
half /hɑːf/
thumb /θʌm/
dialogue /ˈdaɪəlɒg/
scared /skeəd/
tired /ˈtaɪəd/

C. Be particularly careful with **people's names** and **place names**. They may be pronounced very differently from what you expect.

first names	**pronunciation**	**place names**	**pronunciation**
Sean	ʃɔːn	Towcester	ˈtəʊstə
Nigel	ˈnaɪdʒəl	Salcombe	ˈsɔːlkəm
Ian	ɪən	Greenwich	ˈgrenɪtʃ

28 Letters

I. Can you spell your name in English?

II. Match the letters of the alphabet with the words (a-e).

1. 'e' and 'g' rhyme with …	a. 'day'
2. 'i' rhymes with …	b. 'who'
3. 'a' and 'j' rhyme with …	c. 'car'
4. 'r' rhymes with …	d. 'my'
5. 'q' rhymes with …	e. 'tea'

III. Some letters are pronounced like whole words. Match them.

1. b	you
2. c	pea
3. i	bee
4. p	sea
5. r	why
6. t	tea
7. u	eye
8. y	are

IV. Say these abbreviations out loud.

1. CD	4. MI5
2. BBC	5. UFO
3. GB	6. VAT

V. Do you say these pairs of words in the same way or differently? Put a tick in the correct column. ☑

			s	d
1.	he's	his		
2.	your	you're		
3.	juice	shoes		
4.	all	or		
5.	work	walk		

29 Measuring

A. In Britain many people still use a **non-metric system**. When talking about **height** use **'feet'** and **'inches'** rather than 'metres' and 'centimetres'.

He's six feet (foot) two (= six feet and two inches). He's tall.
He's five feet (foot) three (= five feet and three inches). He's short.

B. Remember that the word **'tall'** is **not only** used for **people**.

a tall	man building tree	**but**	a high	wall cliff mountain

C. **Weight** is measured in **pounds** and **stone** (and in the **US** only in **pounds**). One pound is 0.45 kilogram. One stone is 6.35 kilograms. The **abbreviation** for stone is **'st'** and for pound **'lb'**.

She weighs 8 st 10 lb.
He weighs over 15 stone now.

D. **Sizes** for **shoes** and **clothes** are also different.

What size shoes do you take - a 7 or an 8?
What size waist have you got - 32 or 34?
Is that a size 12 dress? No, it's size 14.

E. Talking about **area**.

- *the lounge is fourteen (feet) by nine (feet)*
- *it's fourteen feet long and nine feet wide*
- *5,000 square feet of office space*
- *15 m^2 (= fifteen square metres) of carpet*

F. When **measurements** are used **in front of a noun** you **don't add** 's' to the unit of measurement.

- a ten-mile drive
- a 400-metre race

29 Practice

I. Say how tall you are and how much you weigh. Use feet and inches and stones and pounds. Look at sections A and C.

II. Complete the grid. Six words are missing.

	noun	verb	adjective
1.	the length	...	long
2.	the width	to widen	...
3.	...	to heighten	high
4.	•	to lower	...
5.	•	...	short
6.	the depth	to deepen	...

III. Rewrite these expressions using an adjective with a hyphen.

1. a flat with six rooms
2. a walk which is ten miles long
3. a flight which lasts eight hours
4. an article which stretches over five pages

IV. Read this newspaper article from 1999.

FEET and inches are to be kept in Britain for another 10 years - because America has failed to adopt European Union standards.

The imperial measures were due to disappear at the end of this year when metrication replaced what Brussels calls the 'inch-pound' system across the EU. But industries facing multi-billion pound costs to meet new metric-only labelling laws have won a breathing space until 2009.

Moves to harmonise units of measure began 30 years ago, before Britain joined the EU. Since then, centimetres, metres and kilograms have steadily been taking over - with exceptions such as the mile and the pint of beer. Businesses facing labelling problems were given a reprieve in 1989 and told that imperial units would finally be outlawed from 1999.

But firms dealing in goods from consumer electronics to perfumery have battled on, complaining that they would have to set up two production lines - with EU goods in metric measurements and those going to America in imperial measurements.

Without America ready to convert, the European Commission has agreed to recommend another delay.

30 Money matters

A. Some common words to do with money are difficult **to pronounce**.

receipt	/rɪˈsiːt/	a piece of paper showing that goods have been paid for
debt	/det/	money owed to somebody

B. Remember how these words **combine** with other words **in sentences**.

Can I pay in cash?
Is it OK if I pay by credit card?
Don't go into debt!
Don't forget to get a receipt for your expenses.
Do you pay interest on a current account?

C. Don't confuse these two important verbs.

to lend	**to give** something **to** somebody
to borrow	**to take** something **from** somebody

The banks are lending money at competitive rates of interest.
I want to borrow some money from the bank to buy a car.

D. These are **expressions** you may need **in a bank**.

to pay in instalments:	to pay for something in small portions over many months
a direct debit:	an automatic payment from your account
a standing order:	a fixed payment at regular intervals
a current account:	an account for everyday expenses
a deposit account:	an account for savings
a monthly statement:	a list which shows what went in and out of your account
to pay interest:	to pay money for borrowing money

30 Practice

I. Say these words and expressions out loud. Can you pronounce and stress them properly?

1. cheque
2. turnover
3. a competitive rate of interest
4. a current account

II. Complete these sentences. Use a word from the box.

by ◆ for ◆ in ◆ into ◆ on

1. Is it OK if I pay … cash?
2. I'm going to pay … cheque if you don't mind.
3. How much interest is the bank paying … a deposit account?
4. They went … debt after one of them became redundant.
5. Could you give me a receipt … all this, please?

III. Put in the correct form of 'lend' or 'borrow' to complete these sentences.

1. By the way, thanks for the books you … me last weekend.
2. Would you mind if I … your bike for a few hours?
3. She doesn't like … other people's clothes.
4. Don't … him any money! You won't get it back!
5. How much does it cost to … a book from the local library?

IV. Don't get confused! What's the difference between …

1. 'debt' and 'debit'?
2. a 'form' and a 'formula'?
3. 'expenses' and 'expensive'?
4. 'turnover' and 'turn over'?

V. Look up this word in your dictionary.

Inland Revenue

31 Multi-word verbs

A. **Multi-word verbs** (or **phrasal verbs**) are verbs which have **two** or **more parts**.

We'll drop in on the way home.	(stop for a short visit)
Do you get on with your parents-in-law?	(have a good relationship with)

B. People whose first language is English like multi-word verbs because they are easy to use. All you need is a **simple verb** (eg 'look') and different **particles** (eg 'after', 'for', 'on', 'up', 'with') and you can express a variety of meanings.

She's looking after her grandfather.	(take care of)
Things are looking up.	(improve)
He really looks up to his boss.	(admire)
I'm looking for my key.	(search)

C. There are some **grammatical rules** which you need to understand if you want to use multi-word verbs correctly. You must know, for example, that some multi-word verbs **are separable** and some **are not**.

	type			example
1.	**intransitive**	➔	verb and particle **must stay together**	*We stayed up all night.*
2.	**transitive – separable**	➔	you **can separate** verb and particle; but you **must separate** verb and particle if the **object** (= *light*) is a **pronoun** (= *it*)	*He switched the light on.* *He switched on the light.* *He switched it on.* ~~He switched on it.~~
3.	**transitive – inseparable**	➔	verb and particle **must stay together**	*The dog went for the man.* *The dog went for him.*

D. A good dictionary will give you all the information about multi-word verbs you need. Remember that the **meaning** of these verbs is **not always obvious** from the **individual words**.

Can you fill me in on the plan? (inform me about)

31 Practice

I. These are multi-word verbs. Match them to their 'meanings' (a-f) on the right.

1. Grandma's just dropped off.
2. Do we have to dress up for the party?
3. Don't wait up for me. I'll be very late.
4. He's fallen out with his girlfriend.
5. Her work really stands out, doesn't it?
6. I'll drop in on the way home from work.

a. not go to bed
b. be of high quality
c. visit for a short time
d. put on one's best clothes
e. fall asleep
f. have an argument

II. Write out the sentences below again using the correct form of the multi-word verbs in the box.

break off ◆ dish out ◆ give up ◆ make up ◆ set up ◆ wipe out

1. Can you distribute these letters to the houses in our road?
2. Have you found out who organised the scheme?
3. She has stopped drinking sherry.
4. Do you think he invented that story?
5. She ended their relationship after a month.
6. The bomb destroyed the whole city.

III. Now link the multi-word verbs with their one-word equivalent.

1. Don't worry. We'll stick up for you!
2. It's OK. I'll stand in for you when you're away.
3. Leave it to me. I'll get on to them.
4. Let's get down to business, shall we?
5. She won't put up with behaviour like that.
6. They did away with the law.

a. contact
b. succeed
c. replace
d. tolerate
e. inform
f. abolish
g. support
h. start

32 Music

A. People often **talk about music** and their **tastes in music**.

Do you listen to music?
Are you musical?
Do you play a musical instrument?
How often do you (have to) practise every day?
What sort of music do you like?
Have you heard the new CD by ... ?
What do you think of this?
Can you read music?
Have you got a good sense of rhythm?

B. You probably know these **types of music**.

blues	classical	reggae	rock'n'roll
folk	jazz	soul	techno

C. There are many words for different **instruments**. Here are some of them organised into groups.

string:	cello, violin, harp
keyboard:	piano, harpsichord, synthesiser
brass:	tuba, trumpet, trombone
percussion:	drums, tambourine, maracas
woodwind:	flute, oboe, clarinet

D. Look at this **sequence of events**. Do you know these verbs?

↓ *the music is composed*
↓ *the lyrics are written*
↓ *the songs are rehearsed*
↓ *the songs are recorded*
↓ *the tracks are mixed*
↓ *a master tape is made*
↓ *a CD cover is designed*
↓ *the CDs are produced*

E. Don't mix up these words.

- a 'conductor' conducts an orchestra
- a 'director' directs a film
- a 'single' is one song on a record or CD

32 Practice

I. Which instrument is the odd one out? Say why.

1. flute - trumpet - oboe
2. violin - organ - synthesiser
3. French horn - tuba - kettle drum
4. piano - cello - violin
5. harp - trombone - trumpet
6. harpsichord - violin - harp

II. Which type of music is it?

1. traditional music from a specific region
2. traditional music in the form of a symphony or concerto
3. a type of West Indian music with strong rhythms
4. popular music which started in the US in the early 20th century

III. What's the difference between ...

1. a 'hymn' and a 'ballad'?
2. a 'conductor' and a 'director'?
3. a 'duet' and a 'quartet'?
4. a 'jukebox' and a 'record deck'?

IV. What do we mean when we say ...

1. 'he's got the blues'?
2. 'she's tone deaf'?
3. 'they're on tour in summer'?
4. 'it's a solo album'?

V. Now look up these words in your dictionary.

1. a baton
2. a carol
3. a venue
4. a film score

33 Names and titles

A. In **Britain** and the **US** it is not unusual to use **first names** when **talking to people** you **don't know well**. This is **not** the same as using *'Du'* in German.

- *Hello. My name's Mike.*
- *Pleased to meet you. I'm Diana.*

B. **First names** and **surnames** are common as well.

- *Hello. My name's Mike Lee.*
- *How do you do. I'm Diana Williamson.*

C. What about **surnames on their own**?

Surnames on their own are used when we **talk about public figures** - politicians, sports personalities, writers - but **not** in our day-to-day dealings with **ordinary people**.

D. You can of course use **titles** in English. These sound **formal** or **respectful**. Nowadays many women prefer the title 'Ms' rather than 'Mrs' or 'Miss', especially in business.

title	used when you address ...
Miss /mɪs/ Black	a single woman
Mrs /ˈmɪsɪz/ White	a married woman
Ms /mɪz/ Grey	a single or married woman
Mr /ˈmɪstə/ Green	a single or married man

E. **Academic titles** are only used in **academic** (or **medical**) **environments**. You **cannot** use **'Dr'** with **other forms of address** such as 'Mrs' or 'Prof'.

You say ...	'Mrs Brown'	You **don't** say ...	~~'Mrs Dr Brown'~~
You say ...	'Dr Brown'	You **don't** say ...	~~'Mrs Prof Brown'~~
You say ...	'Professor Brown'	You **don't** say ...	~~'Prof Dr Brown'~~

F. The words **'sir'**, **'madam'** and **'miss'** have special uses in Britain.

- *in **shops** when talking to **customers**:*
  Yes, madam? Can I help you?'
- *in **schools** when children talk to **teachers**:*
  'Please, miss. Can I go to the toilet?'

33 Practice

I. Circle the correct word in the brackets.

1. In Britain people (always - often - never) use first names.
2. In business women often use the title (Mr - Mrs - Ms) nowadays.
3. The title 'Miss' means a woman is (not married - married - under 21).
4. The female equivalent of 'Mr' is ('Mrs' - 'Ms' - 'Miss').
5. If I say 'How are you, John?' to my boss it is saying (*dir* - *euch* - *Ihnen*) to him.

II. 'The done thing' or 'not the done thing' in Britain?
Tick ✓ the correct column.

	action	the done thing	not the done thing
1.	answering the phone by saying your name		
2.	introducing yourself to your neighbour by using your first name		
3.	calling somebody in the office 'Mrs' when you don't know if they are married		
4.	when you're at work calling your boss 'sir'		
5.	saying: 'This is Prof Dr Smith from Bristol'		

III. Where are you when you hear these expressions?

1. 'Sir! Sir! Can I do it, sir? Please!'
2. 'If you could wait one moment, madam, I'll be right with you.'
3. 'I'm sorry, miss. I've left my book at home.'
4. 'Doctor is ready to see you know. Can you come through, please.'
5. 'There's a Mrs Applebloom on the phone. She wants to speak to you.'

34 News and newspaper

A. **Newspapers** can be divided into **several parts**. Here are some you probably know.

business section	cartoons
classified advertisements	crossword
editorial	feature articles
foreign news	headlines
home news	horoscope
letters to the editor	sports

B. In Britain there are a large number of **national newspapers** published daily. People often distinguish between the **popular** and **quality press**.

Popular press (tabloids):	*The Sun*
	The Mirror
	The News of the World
Quality press (broadsheets):	*The Times*
	The Guardian
	The Daily Telegraph

C. **Headlines** in British newspapers often contain **special language** which make them difficult to understand.

PUB BARS FOOTBALL FANS	(to bar = to stop entry)
STUDENTS CLASHED WITH POLICE	(to clash = to fight)
PRINCE CHARLES DUE IN KUWAIT	(due = expected to arrive)
US CUTS AID TO THIRD WORLD	(to cut = to reduce)

D. The English in newspapers is different from other types of English.

Hendrix and Oasis lyrics to be sold

HANDWRITTEN song lyrics by Jimi Hendrix, Oasis and the Spice Girls will be auctioned next month in London.

Three pages of unpublished lyrics and doodles on United Airlines notepaper by Jimi Hendrix in June 1969, the Spice Girls' handwritten lyrics to *Goodbye* and the words to Oasis's *Cast No Shadow* will also be offered for sale by Sotheby's on March 22 ...

34 Practice

I. In which part of a newspaper will you find information about ...

1. the share prices of big companies?
2. football results and an analysis of the games?
3. what readers think about certain subjects?
4. what the newspaper thinks about certain subjects?
5. what's happening in other countries?
6. whether it's going to be a successful day for you or not?

II. Is this text from a tabloid or a quality paper? How do you know?

PARTS of Northern Britain were brought to a standstill by heavy snow and ice yesterday with roads closed and dangerous driving conditions. Scotland was worst hit. Two hundred schools were closed in Aberdeenshire, where roads were impassable, and more than seven inches of snow was recorded at Aberdeen airport.

III. What do these headlines mean? 'Translate' them.

STAR WEDS

PRESIDENT HEADS PEACE MOVES

BOMB BLAST ON US JUMBO

IV. Read these newspaper articles.

No rest for the workers

YOUNG workers are taking fewer and shorter breaks during the day.

Just over half of the 659 25 to 30-year-olds questioned for a British Heart Foundation survey said they took less than 30 minutes for a lunch break.

They also complained that long days in the office prevented them from exercising regularly. A third blamed their job for putting on weight - partly through lack of exercise and also because they ate too many snacks at work.

The survey results will be used in a campaign launched today to make young workers more aware of heart disease. A foundation spokesman said: 'The process of furring up the arteries starts in young people and is influenced by lifestyle.'

The container calamities

ACCIDENTS in the home caused by tins, glass jars and plastic containers cost the NHS more than £12 million a year, says a report.

More than 60,000 Britons are treated in hospital each year after injuring themselves opening or disposing of containers.

Most injuries involve the hands or fingers. One of the most common occurs trying to separate frozen burgers with a knife.

A Government campaign has been launched to cut the number of mishaps by making packages easier to open and safer to use.

Consumer Affairs Minister Kim Howells has published research reports showing how the number of 'container calamities' can be reduced.

35 Numbers

A. Some **cardinal numbers** are difficult **to spell**.

0	nought	15	fifteen
20	twenty	21	twenty-one
30	thirty	40	forty
50	fifty	1,000	a thousand
1,000,000	a million	1,000,000,000	a billion (a thousand million)

B. Some **ordinal numbers** are difficult **to say**.

1st	the first	2nd	the second
3rd	the third	8th	the eighth
20th	the twentieth	21st	the twenty-first

C. There are various words for the **figure 0**.

nought	(general)
zero	(temperature)
oh	(telephone numbers, bank account numbers)
nil	(football, rugby)
love	(tennis)

D. Saying telephone numbers.

Say **each figure separately**, pausing after a group of three (or four). If the same figure comes **twice**, people in Britain say **'double'**.

521837 'five two one - eight three seven'

E. Using **commas** and **full stops**.

Use a **comma** to separate **thousands from hundreds**. A **full stop** (**'point'**) is used for **decimals**.

1,549	'one thousand five hundred and forty-nine'
3.75%	'three point seven five per cent'

35 Practice

I. Write these numbers out as words.

1. 22
2. 84
3. 111
4. 433
5. 1,965

II. Answer it.

How many millions are there in a billion?

III. Say these numbers out loud.

1. 10.5
2. 3,333
3. 438,677
4. 25.6%
5. 56,398,245

IV. Which sport is it?

1. 'Chelsea won three nil.'
2. 'Thirty love. Palfreyman to serve.'
3. 'And the score at half time: Leicester 15, Wasps 24.'

V. Complete these sentences using a number. Write it out in full.

1. Applications will be dealt with on a … come, … served basis.
2. British people have fireworks on the … of November, Guy Fawkes' Night.
3. Did you have a special party on your … birthday?
4. Do you know the expression: '…'s company, …'s a crowd'?
5. Do you think more money should be given to the … World?
6. The normal age of retirement for men is … .
7. The voting age in Britain is … .
8. However, you can drive a car when you're … .

36 Office equipment

A. Modern offices are full of **equipment**. Here are some examples. You should know them.

answerphone	fax machine
scanner	photocopier
desktop PC/laptop	printer
monitor	modem

B. None of the equipment in section A will work without **electricity**. Do you know what these are?

plug
socket
extension lead

C. Offices have **furniture** in them.

bookshelves	cupboard	desk
filing cabinet	swivel chair	table

D. Do you know the following items? You find them in an office.

compliment slips	drawing pins
envelopes	headed notepaper
hole punch	notebook
paper clips	stapler

E. What about these objects? Can you guess what they are?

calculator	date stamp
diary	guillotine
ruler	scales
scissors	sellotape
tray	wastepaper bin

F. See if you have these things on your desk at home.

a sharpener	a rubber
a rubber band	glue
a pencil	a biro

36 Practice

I. What equipment do you need to ...

1. send a document from one office to another very quickly?
2. record telephone messages?
3. make copies of correspondence?
4. type a letter while travelling on a train or plane?
5. get a hard copy of what you have written on your computer?

II. Which words go together?

1. plug	a. noticeboard
2. stamp	b. vase
3. drawing pins	c. envelope
4. coffee	d. socket
5. flowers	e. mug

III. What object from section E is being described?

1. you use them to weigh something
2. you use it for drawing straight lines
3. you use it to remind yourself about appointments
4. you use it for cutting big pieces of paper
5. you use it for keeping your papers in

IV. What's the difference between ...

1. a 'briefcase' and a 'wallet'?
2. a 'diary' and a 'calendar'?
3. a 'date stamp' and a 'stamp'?
4. a 'drawer' and a 'tray'?
5. 'scissors' and a 'guillotine'?

37 People's characters

A. Some **adjectives** to describe people and their characters are **similar** in **German** and **English**. Check the **pronunciation** and **stress**.

sceptical	/ˈskeptɪkəl/	emotional	/ɪˈməʊʃənəl/
aggressive	/əˈgresɪv/	loyal	/ˈlɔɪəl/
creative	/kriːˈeɪtɪv/	talented	/ˈtæləntɪd/

B. Now check these adjectives and their meanings.

adjective	meaning
absent-minded	very forgetful because you are too busy thinking about other things
adventurous	daring and always ready to take risks
amusing	funny; making others laugh
bashful	shy and feeling uncomfortable in social situations
boastful	saying how good you are at something
bright	very clever and able to learn things quickly
calm	not getting excited or nervous about things
cheeky	rude and disrespectful (especially towards people like parents and teachers)
conceited	having a very high opinion of yourself
confident	sure of yourself and your abilities
creative	finding it easy to produce new and original ideas and things
domineering	trying to control others without worrying or caring about how they feel
down-to-earth	very practical and honest
emotional	having strong feelings and easily moved by things
enthusiastic	very interested and excited about something (and this shows in the way you talk or behave)
gullible	easily tricked and tending to believe everything you are told
hospitable	always friendly and welcoming to guests
impatient	hating having to wait for things and not very tolerant of other people's weaknesses
malicious	deliberately trying to hurt or harm others
narrow-minded	finding it hard to accept or understand new or different ideas

37 Practice

Complete this grid. Use the definitions in the box.

always ready to quarrel or attack ◆ hating to lose at anything ◆ with a lot of common sense ◆ selfish and only interested in yourself ◆ taking yourself rather too seriously and thinking you are very important ◆ very brave and not afraid to do dangerous things ◆ very polite ◆ very tolerant of other people's opinions even if they are very different from your own ◆ with a very low opinion of yourself but a high opinion of others

	adjective	**meaning**
1.	aggressive	…
2.	articulate	able to express clearly and effectively your thoughts and feelings
3.	broad-minded	…
4.	charismatic	with personal charm and the power to attract others
5.	competitive	…
6.	considerate	aware of the wishes and needs of others
7.	courageous	…
8.	highly-strung	unusually nervous and easily upset or excited
9.	humble	…
10.	modest	with a lower opinion of yourself than you deserve
11.	pompous	…
12.	rash	very impulsive and not thinking enough about the consequences of your actions
13.	self-centred	…
14.	self-confident	usually sure of your own ability to do things
15.	sensible	…
16.	strong-willed	knowing what you want and able to get it
17.	versatile	with lots of different skills and abilities, able to change from one kind of activity to another
18.	well-mannered	…

38 People's feelings

A. You probably know these words.

bored	calm	disappointed
frustrated	lonely	relaxed

B. Look at these adjectives and their definitions. What is the equivalent in your language?

adjective	meaning
amazed	so surprised that you find it hard to believe what has happened
anxious	feeling very worried and nervous about something that may or may not have happened
bad-tempered	getting angry easily and behaving in a very angry and unfriendly way
cheerful	happy and in good spirits
contented	satisfied and happy with your life
disillusioned	feeling bitter and disappointed because you've lost your belief that someone is good or that an idea or plan is right
fed up	unhappy and feeling dissatisfied or bored
heartbroken	very sad because you have been upset or deeply hurt by something that has happened
humiliated	feeling very ashamed and upset, especially because you've been made to look weak or stupid
irritable	easily annoyed, tending to get angry at small things, often because you already feel bad-tempered about something
miserable	very unhappy
nostalgic	enjoying remembering happy events or experiences from the past, because you are not so happy with your life now
scared	frightened
sceptical	not really believing what other people tell you
sentimental	easily affected by emotions such as sympathy, love or sadness
thrilled	extremely pleased, happy and excited (it could be because you've been told some good news or you are going to do something that you've always wanted to)

38 Practice

Look at these adjectives and what they mean. Then use seven of them to complete the sentences below.

	adjective	meaning
1.	annoyed	feeling slightly angry
2.	apprehensive	worried and nervous about something you're going to do
3.	baffled	completely unable to explain or understand something
4.	complacent	so pleased with your achievements that you don't think there's any need to worry or make an effort
5.	down	feeling sad and depressed
6.	edgy	nervous and likely to lose control
7.	furious	extremely angry
8.	homesick	unhappy because you're away from home
9.	light-headed	finding it hard to think clearly or move steadily
10.	mixed-up	confused and unable to decide what to do
11.	paranoid	convinced that people hate you or that bad things will happen to you (even though this isn't true)
12.	petrified	so frightened that you can't move
13.	resentful	angry and bitter about something you think is unfair
14.	speechless	unable to say anything because you're angry or shocked
15.	touchy	too sensitive and easily offended or annoyed

1. He was … when he heard that someone else had been given the job he had applied for. I don't think I've ever seen him so angry before.
2. We were all … when she told us she was nearly seventy-eight. She really didn't look a day over sixty.
3. They were … when their daughter told them she was expecting a baby.
4. When the mugger put a knife to her throat and asked her to hand over her money she was … .
5. The old lady felt really ... when her dog died. It had been her faithful companion for over ten years.
6. When they first moved to Germany they were very … .They missed Britain, their family and their friends.
7. The young man felt … sitting in the waiting room before his interview.

39 People's looks

A. People come in all **shapes** and **sizes**.

fat	overweight	plump
stout	short	skinny
slim	tall	well-built

B. People like to use more **idiomatic expressions** to describe others.

She's all skin and bones.
He's knee high to a grasshopper.
She's built like a barrel.
He's as round as he is *tall.*

C. People often talk about their (and other people's) **hair**.

form	straight ◆ wavy ◆ curly
colour	fair ◆ grey ◆ dark ◆ strawberry blonde ◆ dyed ◆ redhead (auburn hair)
hair style	with a fringe ◆ with a parting ◆ plaited ◆ tied up

D. And the **face**?

form	round ◆ thin ◆ slim ◆ chubby
colour	dark ◆ fair
marks	with dimples ◆ with freckles ◆ wrinkled ◆ a mole next to her lip ◆ a scar on his cheek

E. Some adjectives can only be used with men or women.

men	**women**	**men and women**
good-looking	beautiful	attractive
handsome	pretty	gorgeous

39 Practice

I. Rewrite these sentences. Use the opposite of the underlined words.

1. She's got <u>curly</u> hair.
2. He's got <u>dark</u> skin.
3. He's <u>tall</u> and <u>thin</u>.
4. She's got <u>long</u> legs and <u>big</u> feet.

II. Put these words into the correct column.

a bit overweight ◆ skinny ◆ short ◆ obese ◆ slim ◆ fat ◆ anorexic ◆ well-built

'positive'	**'negative'**
...	...
...	...
...	...
...	...

III. Look at these adjectives. Which are positive and which are negative?

- elegant
- scruffy
- smart
- untidy
- well-dressed

IV. Look at the ending '-ish'. What does it mean?

- She's got reddish hair.
- He's twenty-fiveish.
- She's tallish.

V. Look up these words in your dictionary. They are all used in connection with hair.

- dandruff
- sideburns
- receding

40 Pubs

A. Here are some **dos** and **dont's** when you're **in a pub** in Britain.

Dos	Dont's
do order drinks at the bar	don't give the bartender a tip
do pay when you order	don't expect the beer to have a head
do go there before 11 pm	don't order 'a beer' (say the name)

B. If you drink **beer** you need to know the **difference** between **'bitter'** and **'lager'**.

- bitter: a type of brown beer with a bitter taste
- lager: a type of light pale beer, served cold

C. What does **'real ale'** mean?

'Real ale' is a general term for all types of beer that are made and stored in a traditional way. Real ale is usually stored in a barrel and cooled in a cellar.

D. When you **ask for beer** you usually say the **name of the beer** (or just **'bitter'** or **'lager'**).

A pint of Pedigree, please.
Two pints of Ruddles County, please.
A pint of Bass and half a pint of London Pride, please.
Three pints of bitter.
A pint of lager.

E. Often people ask for other things at the bar.

Could I have a tray, please?
Have you got any straws?
A packet of salt and vinegar crisps, please.
Oh, I almost forgot. Two packets of peanuts, please!

F. When you go to the pub with other people you often **buy the drinks in 'rounds'** (for the whole group).

What can I get you?
What would you like?
What are you having?
What do you want?
I'll get the next round.
The next one's on me.

40 Practice

I. Read these sentences. Are they right or wrong? Tick your answer.

	R	W
1. 'Lager' and 'bitter' are both types of beer		
2. In pubs you order your drinks and pay for them immediately.		
3. Pubs don't serve food.		
4. You can only drink beer in pubs.		
5. Pubs stay open all night.		
6. Pubs are only for men.		

II. One word is missing. Find it in section D, E or F.

1. If you want to carry a lot of drinks you ask for a … .
2. Children like to drink their drinks out of a … .
3. Half a … of bitter, please.
4. A packet of salt and … crisps, please.
5. Wait a second. It's my turn. I'll get the next … .

III. What do these words rhyme with?

1. tray	a. door
2. darts	b. play
3. straw	c. sail
4. draught	d. hearts
5. ale	e. laughed

IV. Look up the following expressions in your dictionary.

- a soft drink
- a free house
- a local
- a hangover
- a landlord

41 Sport

A. There are so many **different sports**. You probably know most of them in English.

archery	badminton	boxing
cricket	darts	football
golf	hang-gliding	hockey
rowing	rugby	skiing
squash	tennis	windsurfing

B. Don't get confused!

bowls: an outdoor game played on grass
bowling: an indoor game
darts: a singular form (although it has an -s at the end)

C. For many sports you need **special equipment**. Do you know these words? (You hold these objects in your hand.)

golf	-	club	snooker	-	cue
squash	-	racket	hockey	-	stick
cricket	-	bat	archery	-	bow
skiing	-	sticks	rowing	-	oar

D. Some sports can be divided into **separate disciplines**. Look at **athletics**, for example.

running	jumping	throwing
sprints	high jump	discus
middle distance	long jump	javelin
long distance	triple jump	hammer
steeplechase	pole vault	shot put

E. The people who do sport.

people	example
'-er' ending	footballer, swimmer
+ 'player'	tennis player, snooker player
other	cyclist, gymnast

41 Practice

I. Which sport is it? They're all in section A.

1. 'You play it with an egg-shaped ball. It's a popular game in Britain, France and Australia.'
2. 'People often play it in pubs. You need a steady hand and lots of practice!'
3. 'You need to be quite brave to do it. I'm not. I'm scared of heights! The equipment's quite expensive and the weather has to be right, of course!'
4. 'You can only do this where there are mountains and snow. It's a popular sport but there are also people who think it's bad for the environment.'

II. Put the equipment, clothing or places from the box into the correct column in the grid. Use each word only once.

ball ◆ boots ◆ cap ◆ court ◆ gloves ◆ goal ◆ goggles ◆ net ◆ pool ◆ racket ◆ stadium ◆ sticks

football	skiing	swimming	tennis

III. What do you call a person who does the following sports?

1. someone who windsurfs
2. someone who canoes
3. someone who boxes
4. someone who plays hockey
5. someone who does acrobatics
6. someone one who parachutes

IV. Look up this word in your dictionary.

decathlon

42 Stress

A. A **syllable** is a part of a word that **contains a single vowel sound** and that **is pronounced as a unit**.

o O o	o O o	O o o
ex|pen|sive	e|quip|ment	sta|di|um

B. Some words **look** as if they have **three** or **four syllables** but when you say them one of the syllables **'disappears'**.

asp~~i~~rin   secret~~a~~ry   veg~~e~~table

C. In **three-syllable words** you do **not always** stress the **same** syllable.

anyway	O o o
argument	O o o
gallery	O o o
holiday	O o o
Paddington	O o o
timetable	O o o
expensive	o O o
museum	o O o

D. Now look at how these words are stressed.

O o	o O o	O o o	o o O o
pizza	spaghetti	orange juice	conversation
salad	risotto	grandchildren	
waiter	tomato		
menu			

42 Practice

I. One of these words takes the stress on the second syllable (▫□). Which one is it?

biscuit	colour
garden	headache
hungry	later
orange	perhaps
problem	yellow

II. Which words have two syllables and which have three? Put them in the correct box.

afternoon ◆ badminton ◆ basketball ◆ children ◆ dangerous ◆ description ◆ German ◆ homework ◆ letter ◆ trouble

two syllables	three syllables

III. Which syllable is stressed? Put the words in the box into the correct category.

August ◆ birthday ◆ December ◆ disco ◆ invitation ◆ July ◆ party ◆ tomorrow ◆ tonight ◆ youth club

□ ▫	▫ □	▫ □ ▫	▫ ▫ □ ▫

43 Telephoning

A. Types of phone.

a normal phone
a cordless phone
a mobile phone
an answerphone

B. The **parts of a phone**.

button
receiver
dial
mouthpiece
cord
display

C. Talking about **numbers**. Say one number after the other.

The number is 466972. ('four - double six - nine - seven – two')
The code is 0181. ('oh – one – eight – one')
The extension is 319. ('three – one – nine')

D. There are various ways of **answering the phone**. **At home** people **do not** normally say **their names**.

home	business
Hello?	*David speaking.*
927364. Hello?	*David Marsh.*
Good morning.	*David Marsh speaking. Hello?*

E. In Britain the **caller** usually **identifies himself or herself first**.

Hello. This is Paul (here). Can I speak to Jill, please?

F. Some **useful phrases**.

She's not in, I'm afraid. Can I take a message?
Could he ring me back?
Can you give her a message?
Sorry to disturb you.
Thanks for all your help.

43 Practice

I. What's wrong with these sentences? Put them into correct English.

1. *Hello. Alex speaking. Is Jane here, please?
2. *Hello. Can I speak Mr Davidson?
3. *I call you back. OK?
4. *My number is 23 – 45 – 64 – 9.

II. Find the equivalents for sentences 1-5.

1. I'll put you through.	a. Can you speak up, please?
2. Somebody's speaking on that line.	b. I'll ring you later.
3. I can't hear you very well.	c. How're things?
4. How are you?	d. I'll connect you.
5. I'll call you back.	e. The line's busy at the moment.

III. What's your reply? Is it a or b?

1. Sorry, I didn't hear what you said.	a. Sorry. I'll say it again. b. Are you deaf?
2. Could I speak to Rebecca, please?	a. One moment, please. b. Hold.
3. Hello. This is Malcolm Smith here again.	a. Not you again! b. Oh, I remember.
4. Can I leave a message?	a. Of course. b. OK.
5. Thanks for calling.	a. Nevermind. b. Pleasure.

44 The arts

A. 'The arts' is a **general expression**. It means many things.

literature:	novels, poetry, drama
performing arts:	theatre, cinema, ballet, opera, concerts
fine arts:	painting, sculpture

B. The **word 'art'** is usually used in connection with **painting** or **sculpture**. Look at these examples.

We went to an exhibition of African art.
After school he went to art college.
There's a new art gallery in the centre of town.

C. There are other words in this area which often cause problems for learners.

artist:	someone who produces works of art (especially paintings)
artiste:	someone who performs in a show (eg a circus)
classical:	'classical music', 'a classical composer'
classic:	'a classic children's story'

D. Inviting somebody out.

◆ *Would you like to go to the cinema with me?*
◆ *Yes, that'd be nice. What's on?*
◆ *Have you seen the latest James Bond film?*
◆ *No, I haven't. Let's go and watch that.*
◆ *OK. It's on at the Odeon. How about Friday?*
◆ *Fine. What time does it start?*
◆ *Hold on. Let me look. Quarter past eight.*

E. After the performance/show.

◆ *Well? What did you think? I really enjoyed it.*
◆ *Mmm. It was OK but I wouldn't go and see it again.*
◆ *Yeah, I suppose you're right. But the beginning was good, wasn't it?*
◆ *Well, it was like all James Bond films: too many special effects.*
◆ *Don't take it so seriously. It's only a bit of fun!*
◆ *Yeah. I suppose you're right. Let's go and have a drink somewhere.*

44 Practice

I. Cross out the wrong word.

1. 'Alice in Wonderland' is a [classic/classical] children's story.
2. Bach and Mozart are [classic/classical] composers.
3. Should the government provide more money for [art/the arts]?
4. The National Gallery contains some priceless works of [art/arts].

II. Test your knowledge! Which forms of art are the following people associated with?

David Lodge ◆ Edward Elgar ◆ Harold Pinter ◆ Henry Moore ◆ John Constable ◆ Kate Winslet ◆ Margot Fonteyn ◆ William Wordsworth

1.	ballet	
2.	cinema	
3.	classical music	
4.	drama	
5.	novels	
6.	painting	
7.	poetry	
8.	sculpture	

III. Read this information. Can you understand it all?

WYCOMBE SWAN THEATRE

TELEPHONE BOOKINGS
Tickets may be reserved by telephoning but must be paid for by post, by credit card or in person within three working days. Party bookings may be paid for by agreement.

POSTAL BOOKINGS
Cheques should be made payable to Wycombe Swan Theatre and should be accompanied by full booking details and a stamped addressed envelope. Send to:
Box Office, Wycombe Swan, St Mary Street, High Wycombe, Bucks HP11 2XE.

CREDIT CARD BOOKINGS
Access, Visa, Mastercard and Delta are accepted for purchases in person or by telephone. Tickets can be posted first class the next day for a 35p charge or they may be collected from the Box Office.

45 The natural world

A. Look at these dictionary entries. You **don't** use **'the'** with the word **'nature'**.

'They stopped to admire the beauties of nature.'
'Farming on such bad land is a struggle against nature.'
'A sunset is one of the beautiful sights in nature.'

B. You probably know the names of many **animals** in English. Here are some animals that people keep as **pets**.

cat	dog	gerbil
guinea pig	hamster	rabbit

C. If you **go out** you may see these **animals**, **birds** and **insects**.

ant	bee	blackbird	frog
hedgehog	ladybird	mole	pigeon
robin	snail	sparrow	wasp

D. Names of **flowers** can fill whole books. Here are some common ones.

daisy:	has a yellow centre and white leaves; grows in grass
dandelion:	a small wild bright yellow flower; its seeds travel long distances
buttercup:	a very common wild yellow flower that grows in fields
tulip:	grows from a bulb; has a large flower and a tall stem
daffodil:	yellow flower of early spring
crocus:	has single purple, yellow or white flower; opens in early spring
snowdrop:	has a small white flower; appears in early spring

E. Here are some verbs you may not know.

to water flowers	to prune trees (= to shorten branches)
to pick flowers	to feed birds
to mow the lawn	to cut the hedge

45 Practice

I. Link the beginnings and ends of these sentences.

1. A naturalist is	a. the process by which the fittest animals survive.
2. Natural history is	b. a person who studies plants, animals and insects.
3. Natural selection is	c. a route through the countryside.
4. A nature trail is	d. the study of animals and plants.

II. Put the words in the box into the correct column.

beak ◆ nostrils ◆ claw ◆ hoof ◆ mane ◆ paw ◆ tail ◆ whiskers ◆ wing

cat	horse	bird

III. Which animals and birds from section C are being described?

1. ... often get into your house in summer – especially when there are sweet things lying about.
2. ... are dark green so it's sometimes difficult to see them.
3. ... can make holes in your garden.
4. ... can make a mess of your walls and windows.
5. ... can eat your flowers and plants.
6. ... can sting!
7. ... are friendly little birds. They'll eat cheese from your hand.
8. ... sing so beautifully, don't they?

IV. Answer these questions. Use your dictionary.

1. What's an 'endangered species'?
2. What does 'to hibernate' mean?
3. What's a 'daisy chain'?
4. What's the national symbol of England?

46 The time and date

A. There are various ways of **asking for the date**.

What's today's date, please?
What date is it today, please?
What's the date today, please?

B. British and **American** people **say** dates **differently**.

BE	AE
'**the** fifth **of** November'	'November fifth'
'November **the** fifth'	'November five'

C. When you are **talking** about a **year** you say it like this.

'Two thousand and one' (2001)

D. British and **American** people **sometimes write** dates **differently** so to avoid confusion it is advisable to write out the month in full.

	BE	AE
4 December 2001	4.12.01	12.4.01

E. There are also differences in the way people in **Britain** and the **US** **tell the time**.

	BE	AE
3.00	'three (o'clock)'	'three (o'clock)'
3.15	'(a) quarter **past** three'	'(a) quarter **after** three'
3.20	'twenty **past** three'	'twenty **after** three'
3.30	'half (**past**) three'	'half **past** three'
3.45	'(a) quarter **to** four'	'(a) quarter **of** four'

F. The **12-hour clock** or the **24-hour clock** – can I use both?

It is **unusual** to use the **24-hour clock** in **Britain**. If you want to specify what **time of day** it is you just add **'in the morning'**, **'in the afternoon'** or **'in the evening'**. The abbreviations **'am'** and **'pm'** are normally **written** forms only.

46 Practice

I. Say these dates out loud.

1. 31 January
2. 4 April
4. 22 August
5. 9 November

II. Complete this well-known rhyme with four numbers.

'… days has September,
April, June and November,
All the rest have … ,
Except February alone,
Which has but … days clear,
And … in each leap year.'

III. Write down the dates in the British way and the American way.

		BE	AE
1.	7 January 2002		
2.	12 November 2003		
3.	11 December 2006		
4.	5 April 2005		

IV. Look at your diary. When is it - or when was it - this year?

1. New Year's Eve
2. St. Valentine's Day
3. Guy Fawkes' Night
4. St. Patrick's Day
5. Boxing Day

V. What's the time? Say it out loud. (Use the 12-hour clock.)

1. 12.15
2. 3.45
3. 16.25
4. 21.20
5. 3.50
6. 18.35

47 Travel

A. Look at this word grid.

form of transport	vehicle
air	aeroplane, helicopter, glider
rail	fast train, freight train, local train
road	car, motorbike, bus, coach, van, lorry
sea	ferry, hovercraft, yacht, trawler

B. These **parts of a car** have been divided into two groups.

inside the car	outside the car
seatbelt	aerial
accelerator	bonnet
brake	boot
light switch	bumper
clutch	engine
gear lever	exhaust
glove compartment	lights
handbrake	radiator
indicator	wheels
steering wheel	windscreen wipers

C. Buying a **train ticket**.

- *Hello.*
- *Hello. I'd like a return ticket to Birmingham, please.*
- *When are you travelling?*
- *Tomorrow.*
- *And are you coming back on the same day?*
- *Yes.*
- *Will you be leaving after nine in the morning?*
- *Yes, that's right.*
- *OK. That'll be £14.55, please.*
- *Can I pay by credit card?*
- *Yes, of course.*
- *Thanks.*
- *Thank you.*

47 Practice

I. Where do the words in the box go? Fill in the grid.

captain ◆ chauffeur ◆ conductor ◆ pilot ◆ porter ◆ purser ◆ stewardess ◆ ticket collector

form of transport	people
air	
rail	
road	
sea	

II. Which words from section B are missing?

1. The three pedals in a car are the ..., the ... and the ... .
2. You put your luggage in the ... .
3. You use a ... when you park your car on a hill.
4. When you move the ... you show whether you're turning left or right.
5. If it's raining you switch on the ... .
6. You can get better reception on your radio if you pull out the ... .
7. Everyone in a car should wear a ... .
8. Who likes traffic jams when the cars are ... to ... ?

III. Put the words in the box into the text.

baggage reclaim ◆ conveyor belt ◆ customs ◆ flight ◆ departure lounge ◆ duty free shop ◆ screen ◆ security check ◆ taxi ◆ took off ◆ trolley

After passing through a … , where someone looked at our bags, we could go into the … . The first thing we did was to buy some perfume in the … Then we sat down near a television … and waited for our … to be called. Fortunately the plane … on time and an hour and a half later we were back in Germany. We went to the … area and waited for our suitcases. After a few minutes our stuff appeared on the … . We put everything on a … , passed quickly through … and took the first … we could find.

IV. What's the difference between ...

1. a 'van' and a 'lorry'?
2. a 'bus' and a 'coach'?
3. a 'wheel' and a 'steering wheel'?
4. a 'boot' and a 'bonnet'?

48 Verbs with little meaning

A. There are a small group of verbs in English which **do not have** a **clear meaning of their own**. Most of the meaning is in the noun that follows the verb. **Verb + noun structures** like these are very widely used by English-speaking people.

B. Read these examples with **'have'**.

Before booking his holiday he had a look through some brochures.
First she read the paper and then she had a swim in the sea.
They sat on the bench and had a chat.

C. Another verb like this is **'take'**.

She took a shower and went to bed.
He took a photograph of us outside Buckingham Palace.
Can I take a look at your new computer?

D. **'Make'** is also a common verb in English.

We made some enquiries into the cost of new central heating.
She made a speech about learning to deal with stress.
During the meal he made a comment about the food.

E. Now look at the way **'give'** is used.

He gave a sigh, shook his head and left the room.
She gave us a terrible glance when she heard us talking about her.
They gave us a humorous account of their first trip to Scotland.

F. Often there is a **more formal equivalent** of these verb + noun structures.

They sat on the bench and chatted.
Can I look at your new computer?
During the meal he commented on the food.
He sighed, shook his head and left the room.

48 Practice

I. Make these sentences sound more informal. Use a verb + noun structure. (You may have to make some other small changes, too.)

1. I rode on my friend's motorbike.
2. In the afternoon we walked into the village.
3. They drank a beer before they went out.
4. She danced with her father first.

II. Do the opposite now and make these sentences more formal. (Again, you may have to make some other small changes.)

1. They took the decision to close one of the factories.
2. Let's take a break, shall we?
3. She wants to take a day off next week.
4. He took a deep breath and jumped into the swimming pool.

III. What word is missing? The first two letters are given.

1. She made a good im... on them. They gave her the job.
2. Can I make a su...? – Yes, please do! What is it?
3. I was very quiet. Really! I didn't make a so... .
4. They made an ef... but it wasn't really good enough.

IV. One verb is missing. Is it 'have' or 'make' or 'give'?

1. I can ... you some advice if you want.
2. Here's the question. Can you ... me the answer?
3. She ... a reason for her behaviour but nobody believed her.
4. This is our opinion. Would you like to ... us your opinion?

V. Which use of 'take' in these four sentences has little meaning?

1. He's taking Chemistry at university.
2. Why do you always take offence when I make a suggestion?
3. The journey took us ten hours.
4. The policemean took down my name and address.

Now look up the verb 'take' in your dictionary.
How many pages of meanings does it contain?

49 Word pairs

A. What are word pairs?

Word pairs (sometimes called **'binomials'**) are informal expressions where **two words** are **joined by 'and'**. The **order** of the words is usually **fixed**.

A black and white film, please.
Hello, boys and girls. Welcome to the show!

B. Often it's quite easy to remember the **sound** of a word pair.

They have to wine and dine with important customers.	(entertain)
This is where you can put your bits and bobs.	(small items)

C. Many **small grammatical words** make up word pairs, too.

He's feeling better now, and is out and about again.	(going out)
She cycled up and down the street.	(in both directions)

D. Sometimes the words in the pair have a **similar meaning**.

Isn't it nice to have some peace and quiet at last?	(peace/calm)
First and foremost, you must pass your exams.	(most importantly)

E. Some word pairs are **not linked** by 'and'.

You've got your jumper on back to front.	(the wrong way)
Sooner or later, you'll know what I mean.	(one day)

49 Practice

I. Complete these sentences. Use the word pairs in the box.

back and forth ◆ here and there ◆ on and off ◆ rack and ruin ◆ rough and ready

1. The old cottage has gone to ... . It's a pity, isn't it?	(ruined)
2. The hotel was a bit ... but very cheap.	(poor standard)
3. Oxford's a big place and there are cafés	(scattered round)
4. I've been writing this letter ... all weekend.	(occasionally)
5. I'm tired. I've been running ... all day!	(to and from somewhere)

II. What do these word pairs mean? Link the meaning (a-e) to the sentence (1-5).

a. large steps
b. gradually
c. choose from a wide selection
d. shouting angrily
e. survive or fail

1. His mother was <u>ranting and raving</u> at him.
2. You can <u>pick and choose</u>; it's up to you.
3. Your English is progressing in <u>leaps and bounds</u>.
4. Her parents won't help her; she'll just have to <u>sink or swim</u>.
5. <u>Slowly but surely</u>, I realised the boat was sinking.

III. Join the words in the two lists to make a pair.

1. law and …	a. then
2. now and …	b. foremeost
3. hit and …	c. cold
4. odds and …	d. gentlemen
5. first and …	e. order
6. peace and ...	f. ends
7. ladies and …	g. quiet
8. hot and …	h. miss

IV. Can you understand these sentences? If not, use your dictionary!

1. He didn't want to be just friends with her; it had to be <u>all or nothing</u>.
2. Well, I'm very sorry but that's all I can offer you; <u>take it or leave it</u>.
3. I think it's sixty miles to the sea, <u>give or take</u> a few miles.

50 Words you can confuse

A. Some words are easy to confuse. Look at these examples.

◆ diary - calendar
I'll write down the appointment in my diary.
According to the calendar on the kichten wall there are five weeks until Christmas.

◆ raise - rise
Raise your hand if you think that the office staff should get more money.
Does the sun rise in the east or the west?

◆ price - prize
The price of petrol has gone up by 5% in the last six months.
She won a prize for coming first.

◆ lend - borrow
The bank refused to lend him the money.
He borrowed some money from his brother.

◆ economic - economical
We're not going to expand until the economic situation has improved.
It's a small car and very economical.

◆ cause - reason
What was the cause of the argument?
There is no reason for you to be so angry.

◆ take - bring
Can you take us to the station?
I'll bring you the photographs tomorrow.

◆ personal - personnel
Please bring a personal data sheet with you.
Your interview will be with the personnel manager.

◆ principal - principle
The principal of the school is Mrs Elizabeth Barton.
It's one of our principles not to smoke in front of children.

◆ stationary - stationery
Don't touch the conveyor belt until it is stationary.
Can you get me some glue from the stationery cupboard?

50 Practice

I. Cross out the wrong word in each pair of brackets.

1. How will the increase in interest rates [affect/effect] your business?
2. My bank manager has agreed to [borrow/lend] me another £2,000.
3. We've had to [cancel/postpone] the meeting until next Wednesday.
4. These machines are [controlled/inspected] at least once a day.
5. My plane was [delayed/postponed] by an hour due to bad weather.
6. I am [interested/interesting] in their new laptop.
7. She applied for a [job/work] at the bank.
8. Some people have a long [journey/travel] to work every day.
9. The cost of [life/living] has gone up again.
10. Please send precise [measurements/measures] when you order.
11. We expect prices to [raise/rise] by at least five per cent this year
12. We only exchange goods if you produce a [receipt/recipe].

II. Which word fits best into the gap – a, b or c?

1. We're going to ask our bank manager for some ... on buying a house.
   a) advice b) advise c) aid
2. We ... each new delivery very carefully.
   a) control b) test c) check
3. She enclosed a ... slip with the catalogue.
   a) complement b) greetings c) compliment
4. Hey! You shouldn't read ... documents!
   a) private b) confident c) confidential
5. He's normally a very ... worker but he's got very lazy recently.
   a) conscientious b) conscious c) conservative
6. The unions criticised the government's ... policy.
   a) economic b) economical c) economics
7. She took her case to an ... tribunal and won.
   a) industrial b) industrious c) illustrious
8. Please send me your latest catalogue and ... list.
   a) pricing b) prize c) price

Key

1 Practice

I. All these dictionaries are good.

II. An almond is a nut which you can eat or use when you are cooking. - Garlic is like an onion. It has a very strong smell and taste. - You use flour to make bread and cakes.

III. The ‘n’ means the word is a noun. The ‘[U]’ means the word is uncountable.

IV. The words ‘flour’ and ‘flower’ are pronounced in the same way: /ˈflaʊə/

V. The word ‘diet’ means *Diät* and *Ernährung* in German.

VI. **1.** b. - **2.** d. - **3.** a. - **4.** c.

VII. **enjoy** = verb - **books** = noun - **but** = conjunction - **speaking** = gerund

2 Practice

I. **1.** although - **2.** cup of tea - **3.** game - **4.** furniture - **5.** page - **6.** scissors
7. stomach - **8.** traffic jam

II.

❐ **❐** ❐ ❐	❐ **❐** ❐ ❐	**❐** ❐ ❐	**❐** ❐
1. binoculars	**2.** capacity	**3.** fashionable	**4.** greenhouse
❐ ❐	❐ **❐**	**❐** ❐ ❐	**❐** ❐
5. muscle	**6.** unless	**7.** vegetables	**8.** vineyard

III. **1.** bike - **2.** phone - **3.** paper - **4.** bye - **5.** lab

IV. **1.** Don’t smoke in the theatre. - **2.** If you drop litter then you have to pay £200. - **3.** If you steal from this shop you can go to court (and prison). - **4.** Don’t give food to the horses.

3 Practice

I. These are all useful ways of remembering words.

II. **1.** b) - **2.** a) - **3.** b) - **4.** b)
This quiz shows us that it is impossible - and not necessary - to learn all the words in the English language.

4 Practice

I. list 3 (These are ‘grammar words’ and not ‘content words’.)

II. **1.** white - **2.** blue - **3.** black - **4.** white - **5.** red - **6.** yellow

5 Practice

I. **1.** impossible - **2.** insecure - **3.** intolerant - **4.** unhappy - **5.** irrelevant - **6.** illegible
II. **1.** to unwrap - **2.** to disappear - **3.** to disbelieve - **4.** to dislike - **5.** to unplug - **6.** to displease
III. **1.** CD player - **2.** cooker - **3.** coffee grinder - **4.** translator - **5.** dishwasher - **6.** actor
IV. *Scheibenwischer - Vergaser - Kühler - Tacho*
V. **1.** competition - **2.** donations - **3.** reduction - **4.** complications - **5.** revolutions - **6.** investigation

6 Practice

I. **1.** a - **2.** are - **3.** pairs - **4.** were - **5.** them - **6.** are, are
II. **1.** f. - **2.** d. - **3.** b. - **4.** a. - **5.** c. - **6.** e.
III.

men	women	men and women
braces	blouse	coat
shirt	dress	gloves
tie	knickers	jacket
underpants	skirt	socks

IV. **1.** e. - **2.** f. - **3.** a. - **4.** b. - **5.** d. - **6.** c.
V. This expression means ‘calm down’.

7 Practice

I. **1.** request - **2.** order - **3.** order
II. b. The verbs are in the past tense.
III. **1.** ..., did we ? - **2.** ..., have you? - **3.** ..., isn’t he? - **4.** ..., couldn’t they? **5.** ..., didn’t she? - **6.** ..., am I?
IV. All these sentences are correct.

8 Practice

(See also The Business World, Module 9A)

I. **1.** ... bowl ... . - **2.** ... box ... . - **3.** ... jars. - **4.** ... bowls ... - **5.** ... mugs. - **6.** ... ‘can’ ... ‘tin’ ... . - **7.** ... pint (= bottle) ... ? - **8.** ... packet ... !
II. **1.** a pack of cards; a packet of biscuits - **2.** a glass of water; a jar of jam **3.** a box of matches; a carton of cream - **4.** a mug of tea; a jug of water

III. **1.** a packet of crisps - **2.** a mug of hot chocolate - **3.** a bottle of lemonade - **4.** a jug of cream

IV. **1.** A bottle is usually made of glass (or plastic). - **2.** A barrel is usually made of wood. - **3.** A bucket is usually made of metal (or plastic). - **4.** A pack is usually made of paper. - **5.** A tin is usually made of metal. **6.** A jar is usually made of glass.

9 Practice

I. In Germany people write their names at the top of letters. They also put their address on the left of the page and not on the right as in Britain.

II.

43 Bridge Street
Royston
Buckinghamshire
HP16 9QP
4 February 20..

Dear John and Joan

Thanks very much for dinner yesterday. We really enjoyed it. Can Joan give us the recipe for the lasagne?

Mark and I are planning a weekend in Wales in March. Would you like to come with us? We would leave on Friday and come back on Sunday and stay at a B&B somewhere. Give us a ring if you're interested and we can sort out the details.

Thanks once again. See you soon.

Love

Susan and Mark

PS Did I leave my gloves at your place? I couldn't find them when I got back home.

10 Practice

I.

country	adjective	country	adjective
Argentina	Argentinian	Japan	Japanese
China	Chinese	Korea	Korean
Greece	Greek	Mexico	Mexican
The Netherlands	Dutch	Norway	Norwegian
Israel	Israeli	Turkey	Turkish

II. Northern Ireland

III.

German	English
Wien	Vienna
Nürnberg	Nuremberg
Bodensee	Lake Constance
Köln	Cologne
Donau	Danube
Schwarzwald	The Black Forest

11 Practice

I. **1.** book a table - **2.** go to the restaurant - **3.** sit down - **4.** read the menu **5.** order the food and drinks - **6.** have the starter - **7.** have the main course - **8.** order the dessert - **9.** ask for the bill - **10.** pay the bill - **11.** leave a tip for the waiter - **12.** leave the restaurant

II.

starter	main course	dessert
melon	chicken casserole	apple fritters
prawn cocktail	roast duck	chocolate mousse
tomato soup	trout	peach melba

12 Practice

(See also Fast Track, Modules 1B, 26A, 26B, 26C)

III. **1.** I ~~learned~~ (= revised) for my exams and passed them all.
IV. **1.** c. - **2.** d. - **3.** a. - **4.** b.
V. **1.** e. - **2.** b. - **3.** c. - **4.** a. - **5.** d.

13 Practice

I.

kitchen	bathroom	lounge
cooker	electric razor	video recorder
dishwasher	hairdryer	hi-fi
freezer	electric toothbrush	television

II. **2.** ... to boil water. - **3.** ... to clean carpets (or floors). - **4.** ... to heat (or defrost) food. - **5.** ... to keep food cool. - **6.** ... to play CDs, cassettes or records.
III. **1.** ... set ...? - **2.** ... switch off ... . - **3.** ... change ... . - **4.** ... empty ... . - **5.** ... touch ... . - **6.** ... recharge ... .

IV. **1.** ... hammer ... nail. - **2.** ... axe. - **3.** ... saw. - **4.** ... spanner. - **5.** ... pliers. **6.** ... sandpaper.

14 Practice

I.

AE	BE	AE	BE
vacation	holiday	gas	petrol
elevator	lift	cookies	biscuits
sidewalk	pavement	fall	autumn

II.

AE	BE	AE	BE
to practice	to practise	liter	litre
tire	tyre	defense	defence
humor	humour	check	cheque

III. **1.** a) - **2.** b) - **3.** a) - **4.** c) - **5.** a)

15 Practice

I. **1.** boss - **2.** mustn't - **3.** opinion - **4.** eventually

II. **1.** handy - **2.** actually - **3.** getting - **4.** slip-on-shoes

III.

	German	English
1.	*spenden*	donate
2.	*Unternehmer*	person in business
3.	*Chef*	boss
4.	*Kritik*	criticism
5.	*Gift*	poison
6.	*sympathisch*	nice

IV.

	German	English
1.	*Turnhalle*	gymnasium
2.	*gewöhnlich*	ordinary
3.	*Passierschein*	pass
4.	*Werbung*	promotion
5.	*Schnalle*	buckle
6.	*untersuchen*	to probe

16 Practice

(See also Fast Track, Module 3A)

I.

male	female
nephew	niece
brother	aunt
father	daughter
grandfather	grandmother
son	mother
uncle	sister

II. **1.** ... sister. - **2.** ... brother. - **3.** ... father. - **4.** ... mother. - **5.** ... grandfather. - **6.** ... grandmother. - **7.** ... aunt. - **8.** ... uncle.

III. **1.** ... can't stand ... . - **2.** ... fallen out ... . - **3.** ... broken up. - **4.** ... made up ... . - **5.** ... hit it off ... !

17 Practice

(See also Fast Track, Modules 5A, 5B, 5D)

I.

fruit	vegetable
apricot	asparagus
melon	cauliflower
lemon	celery
orange	courgette
strawberry	leek

II.

from a pig:	*pork*	*ham*	bacon
from a sheep:	*lamb*	mutton	
from a calf:	veal		

III. **1.** 'Bitter' is not the same as 'lager'; bitter is darker, warmer and more bitter than lager. - **2.** 'Apple juice' doesn't have alcohol in it; 'cider' does. - **3.** (the same) - **4.** An 'old wine' is simply old. A 'vintage wine' is an old wine of high quality.

IV. **1.** ... pepper - **2.** ... fork - **3.** ... sugar - **4.** ... tonic - **5.** ... chips - **6.** ... butter

VI. lettuce = 'let us'

18 Practice

(See also Fast Track, Module 14A; The Business World, Modules 2B, 5B, 8B, 9B)

I. **1.** f. - **2.** e. - **3.** a. - **4.** g. - **5.** h. - **6.** c. - **7.** b. - **8.** d.

II. **1.** ... sneezes loudly ... - **2.** ... wins a prize ... - **3.** ... would like to go through a door in front of you ... - **4.** ... is disappointed ... - **5.** ... feels that you have disturbed them ... - **6.** ... talks too quietly ... - **7.** ... wants to use your phone to make a quick call ... - **8.** ... says 'thank you' ...

III. **e.** John! Hi! What are you doing here? - **c.** Hi. I was in the area so I thought I'd see if you were in. - **b.** Great! Come in. - **h.** Thanks. I won't stay long. **a.** Cup of coffee? - **g.** Oh, that'd be lovely. It's a bit chilly outside. - **d.** Is it? I haven't been out today. Sugar? - **f.** No, thanks. Just milk.

19 Practice

(See also Fast Track, Module 11A)

I. **1.** e. - **2.** c. - **3.** d. - **4.** a. - **5.** b.

II. **1.** f. - **2.** c. - **3.** g. - **4.** a. - **5.** h. - **6.** e. - **7.** b. - **8.** d.

III.

Drinking lots of water	✓
Getting a good night's sleep	✓
Eating chips and ketchup	×
Drinking beer every day	×
Getting plenty of exercise	✓

20 Practice

I.

you can do it alone	you must do it with another person
listening to music	going for a drink with friends
photography	having flying lessons
playing an instrument	playing chess
reading	parachuting
stamp collecting	water skiing

II. **1.** golf - **2.** swimming (indoors) - **3.** cycling

III. **1.** cards - **2.** chess - **3.** Monopoly - **4.** golf

21 Practice

(See also Fast Track, Modules 2A, 2C, 9B, 10A, 10B, 12B; The Business World, Modules 6A, 6B)

I. **1.** self-catering accommodation - **2.** bed and breakfast - **3.** timc-share apartment - **4.** youth hostel
II. **1.** sunbathing - **2.** swimming (in the sea) - **3.** doing nothing special - **4.** sightseeing
III. a hotel

22 Practice

(See also Fast Track, Modules 15A, 15C, 15E; The Business World, Module 11B)

I.

kitchen	lounge	study	bathroom	all rooms
cutlery	CDs	computer	razor	floor and ceiling
dishwasher	settee	encyclopaedia	toothbrush	light switch
tin opener	video recorder	envelopes	towel	power point

II. **1.** dining room - **2.** conservatory - **3.** study - **4.** hall
III. **1.** A 'chair' is not as large or as comfortable as an 'armchair'. - **2.** You hang clothes up in a 'wardrobe'. In a 'chest of drawers' you keep smaller items of clothing like socks or underwear. - **3.** A 'desk' is in an office or a school. It usually has drawers. A 'table' is a more general word. - **4.** A 'hall' is downstairs in a house. A 'landing' is upstairs.
IV. **1.** ... bunk beds. - **2.** ... shed ... - **3.** Double glazing ... - **4.** ... lawns ...
V. **1.** *freistehendes Haus* - **2.** *Doppelhaushälfte* - **3.** *Reihenhaus*

23 Practice

(See also Fast Track and The Business World, Modules D)

I. positive
II. He's feeling a bit sick. - She's very well indeed.
III. The other person is talking all the time! - They are always talking about their work!
IV. relax - go to bed
V. **1.** d. - **2.** f. - **3.** e. - **4.** b.

24 Practice

(See also The Business World, Modules 12A, 12B, 12C)

1. b. - **2.** b. - **3.** b. - **4.** b. - **5.** b. - **6.** a. - **7.** c. - **8.** b. - **9.** d. - **10.** a. - **11**. b. - **12.** c.

25 Practice

(See also Fast Track, Modules 6C, 10C, 12A; The Business World, Modules 1A, 7A - 7E, 10A)

I. **1.** *Was machst du/machen Sie gerade?* - **2.** *Was machst du/machen Sie beruflich?*

II. **1.** A secretary because a secretary doesn't wear a uniform. - **2.** A priest because a priest doesn't work with his/her hands. - **3.** A politician because a politician doesn't 'create' something. - **4.** A teacher because a teacher's job doesn't have anything to do with animals.

III. **1.** to be without a job - **2.** to apply for a job - **3.** to be invited for an interview - **4.** to be offered a job - **5.** to accept a job offer - **6.** to start a new job **7.** to work hard - **8.** to be given a pay rise - **9.** to be made redundant

26 Practice

(See also Fast Track, Modules 21A, 21B; The Business World, Modules 12A-12D)

I.

be	do	have
2	1	4
3	5	6

II. **1.** We're all getting older, aren't we? - **2.** We got a postcard from Don yesterday. - **3.** We got home in the middle of the night. - **4.** Can you get some stamps for me on your way home? - **5.** Do you get this question? I don't know what it means! - **6.** Could you get my wallet from the kitchen, please?

III. **1.** e. - **2.** d. - **3.** b. - **4.** a. - **5.** f. - **6.** c.

27 Practice

I. **1.** j. - **2.** e. - **3.** i. - **4.** c. - **5.** h. - **6.** l. - **7.** f. - **8.** g. - **9.** n. - **10.** a. - **11.** m. - **12.** o. - **13.** k. - **14.** b. - **15.** d.

II. **1.** manslaughter - **2.** murder - **3.** shoplifting

28 Practice

(See also Fast Track, Modules 15B; The Business World, Modules 1B, 4A-4E, 13A-13C)

II. **1.** e. - **2.** d. - **3.** a. - **4.** c. - **5.** b.

III. **1.** b./bee - **2.** c./sea - **3.** i./eye - **4.** p./pea - **5.** r./are - **6.** t./tea - **7.** u./you **8.** y./why

V. **1.** differently - **2.** same - **3.** differently - **4.** differently - **5.** differently

29 Practice

(See also Fast Track, Module 5E)

II.

	noun	verb	adjective
1.	the length	to lengthen	long
2.	the width	to widen	wide
3.	the height	to heighten	high
4.	•	to lower	low
5.	•	to shorten	short
6.	the depth	to deepen	deep

III. **1.** a six-room flat - **2.** a ten-mile walk - **3.** an eight-hour flight - **4.** a five-page article

30 Practice

I. **1.** /tʃek/ - **2.** /ˈtɜːnˌəʊvə/ - **3.** /ə kəmˈpetətɪv ˈreɪtəv ˈɪntrəst/ - **4.** /ə ˌkʌrənt əˈkaʊnt/

II. **1.** in - **2.** by - **3.** on - **4.** into - **5.** for

III. **1.** lent - **2.** borrowed - **3.** borrowing - **4.** lend - **5.** borrow

IV. **1.** A 'debt' is when you owe somebody money. A 'debit' is a sum of money which is taken out of your bank account. - **2.** A 'form' is a piece of paper you fill in. A 'formula' is an expression used in a subject like chemistry. For example H_2O is the formula for water. - **3.** Your 'expenses' is the money you need when you do a certain job. People say 'travelling expenses', for example. If something is 'expensive' it costs a lot of money. - **4.** 'Turnover' is the amount of money a company takes in. If you 'turn over' something, such as a page, you turn it so that you can see the other side.

V. *Finanzamt*

31 Practice

I. **1.** e. - **2.** d. - **3.** a. - **4.** f. - **5.** b. - **6.** c.
II. **1.** dish out - **2.** set up - **3.** given up - **4.** made up - **5.** broke off - **6.** wiped out
III. **1.** g. - **2.** c. - **3.** a. - **4.** h. - **5.** d. - **6.** f.

32 Practice

(See also Fast Track, Modules 8A -8E, 17D)

I. **1.** A trumpet is not a woodwind instrument. - **2.** A violin does not have a keyboard. - **3.** A kettle drum is not a brass instrument. - **4.** A piano is not a string instrument. - **5.** A harp is not a brass instrument. - **6.** A harpsichord is not a string instrument.
II. **1.** folk - **2.** classical - **3.** reggae - **4.** jazz
III. **1.** A 'hymn' is a religious song. A 'ballad' is a song which tells a story. **2.** A 'conductor' conducts an orchestra. A 'director' directs a film. - **3.** A 'duet' is two people singing or playing musical instruments together. A 'quartet' is four people performing music or singing together. **4.** A 'jukebox' is a machine in a pub or club which plays the music you want when you put in money. A 'record deck' is a platform where you put records before you can play them.
IV. **1.** he's sad - **2.** she can't sing (because she can't tell the difference between different musical notes) - **3.** they're performing on stage in different towns and cities - **4.** an album performed by an individual (and not a group)
V. **1.** *Taktstock* - **2.** *Weihnachtslied* - **3.** *Veranstaltungsort* - **4.** *Filmmusik*

33 Practice

I. **1.** often - **2.** Ms - **3.** not married - **4.** 'Ms' - **5.** *Ihnen*
II. **1.** not the done thing - **2.** the done thing - **3.** not the done thing - **4.** not the done thing - **5.** not the done thing
III. **1.** school - **2.** shop - **3.** school - **4.** doctor's practice - **5.** office

34 Practice

(See also Fast Track, Modules 22A, 22C)

I. **1.** business section - **2.** sports section - **3.** letters to the editor - **4.** editorial **5.** foreign news - **6.** horoscope

II. The article is from a quality paper. It contains long sentences.

III. A famous person has got married. - The president himself/herself is taking responsibility for reaching an agreement in the peace talks. - A bomb has exploded on board a US jumbo jet.

35 Practice

I. **1.** twenty-two - **2.** eighty-four - **3.** a (= one) hundred and eleven - **4.** four hundred and thirty-three - **5.** one thousand, nine hundred and sixty-five

II. a thousand

III. **1.** 'ten point five' - **2.** 'three thousand, three hundred and thirty-three' - **3.** 'four hundred and thirty eight thousand, six hundred and seventy-seven' **4.** 'twenty-five point six per cent' - **5.** 'fifty-six million, three hundred and ninety-eight thousand, two hundred and forty-five'

IV. **1.** football - **2.** tennis - **3.** rugby

V. **1.** ... first ... , first ... . - **2.** ... fifth ... . - **3.** ... eighteenth ...? - **4.** ... two ..., three ...? - **5.** ... Third ...? - **6.** ... sixty-five. - **7.** ... eighteen. - **8.** ... seventeen.

36 Practice

(See also Fast Track, Modules 25A, 25B; The Business World, Modules 3B, 3D, 8A)

I. **1.** fax - **2.** answerphone - **3.** photocopier - **4.** laptop - **5.** printer

II. **1.** d. - **2.** c. - **3.** a. - **4.** e. - **5.** b.

III. **1.** scales - **2.** ruler - **3.** diary - **4.** guillotine - **5.** tray

IV. **1.** A 'briefcase' is a bag for keeping books, files and papers in. A 'wallet' is what men carry in their inside pockets. It contains things like (paper) money, a driving licence or credit cards. - **2.** A 'diary' is a small book in which you keep a record of appointments or the things you have done. A 'calendar' hangs on the wall and shows you the days of the month. Often each month is shown with a photograph. - **3.** A 'date stamp' is used in offices to record when a letter arrived and was opened. A 'stamp' is put on a letter before it is posted. - **4.** A 'drawer' is part of a desk. You keep papers and pens in it. A 'tray' is used for keeping papers together on your desk. People talk about an 'in-tray' and an 'out-tray', for example. (A tray can also be used for carrying cups, glasses and plates on.) - **5.** You use 'scissors' to cut a piece of paper. You use a 'guillotine' to cut a pile of paper.

37 Practice

	adjective	meaning
1.	aggressive	always ready to quarrel or attack
3.	broad-minded	very tolerant of other people's opinions even if they are very different from your own
5.	competitive	hating to lose at anything
7.	courageous	very brave and not afraid to do dangerous things
9.	humble	with a very low opinion of yourself but a high opinion of others
11.	pompous	taking yourself rather too seriously and thinking you are very important
13.	self-centred	selfish and only interested in yourself
15.	sensible	with a lot of common sense
18.	well-mannered	very polite

38 Practice

1. furious - **2.** baffled - **3.** speechless - **4.** petrified - **5.** down - **6.** homesick **7.** apprehensive

39 Practice

I. **1.** straight - **2.** fair - **3.** short, fat. - **4.** short, small

II.

'positive'	'negative'
a bit overweight	skinny
short	obese
slim	fat
well-built	anorexic

III. elegant = positive - scruffy = negative - smart = positive - untidy = negative - well-dressed = positive

IV. The suffix -ish means 'almost', 'approximately', 'something close to'

V. *Schuppen* - *Koteletten* - his hair is receding: *er hat eine leichte Stirnglatze*

40 Practice

(See also Fast Track, Modules 14A-14E)

I. **1.** right - **2.** right - **3.** wrong - **4.** wrong - **5.** wrong - **6.** wrong

II. **1.** ... tray. - **2.** ... straw. - **3.** ... pint ... . - **4.** ... vinegar ... . - **5.** ... round.

III. **1.** b. - **2.** d. - **3.** a. - **4.** e. - **5.** c.

IV. A soft drink does not contain alcohol. - A free house is a pub which is not linked to a specific brewery. - A local is the pub you go to regularly. A hangover is the feeling you have when you get up in the morning after you've drunk too much. - A landlord is the person who runs a pub.

41 Practice

(See also Fast Track, Modules 7A -7E, 11A-C, 19C)

I. **1.** rugby - **2.** darts - **3.** hang-gliding - **4.** skiing

II.

football	**skiing**	**swimming**	**tennis**
ball	boots	cap	court
goal	gloves	goggles	net
stadium	sticks	pool	racket

III. **1.** windsurfer - **2.** canoeist - **3.** boxer - **4.** hockey player - **5.** acrobat - **6.** parachutist

IV. decathlon = *Zehnkampf*

42 Practice

I. perhaps

II.

two syllables	**three syllables**
children	afternoon
German	badminton
homework	basketball
letter	dangerous
trouble	description

III.

□ ▫	▫ □	▫ □ ▫	▫ ▫ □ ▫
August	July	December	invitation
birthday	tonight	tomorrow	
disco			
party			
youth club			

43 Practice

I. **1.** Hello. Alex speaking. Is Jane <u>there</u>, please? - **2.** Hello. Can I speak <u>to</u> Mr Davidson? - **3.** I'<u>ll</u> call you back. OK? - **4.** My number is <u>2345649</u>.

II. **1.** d. - **2.** e. - **3.** a. - **4.** c. - **5.** b.

III. **1.** a. - **2.** a. - **3.** b. - **4.** a. - **5.** b.

44 Practice

(See also Fast Track, Modules 16A, 16B, 16D, 17A, 17C; The Business World 2C)

I. **1.** classic - **2.** classical - **3.** the arts - **4.** art

II.

1.	ballet	Margot Fonteyn
2.	cinema	Kate Winslet
3.	classical music	Edward Elgar
4.	drama	Harold Pinter
5.	novels	David Lodge
6.	painting	John Constable
7.	poetry	William Wordsworth
8.	sculpture	Henry Moore

45 Practice

(See also Fast Track, Modules 15C, 24A-D)

I. **1.** b. - **2.** d. - **3.** a.- **4.** c.

II.

cat	horse	bird
paw	nostrils	beak
tail	hoof	claw
whiskers	mane	wing

III. **1.** Ants - **2.** Frogs - **3.** Moles - **4.** Pigeons - **5.** Snails - **6.** Wasps - **7.** Robins - **8.** Blackbirds

IV. **1.** It's an animal or bird which is in danger of dying out. - **2.** It means to sleep through the winter. - **3.** It's a chain made of daisies. (Small children like to make them.) - **4.** It's a rose.

46 Practice

I. **1.** 'the thirty-first of January' - **2.** 'the fourth of April' - **4.** 'the twenty-second of August' - **5.** 'the ninth of November'

II. 'Thirty days has September,
April, June and November,
All the rest have thirty-one,
Except February alone,
Which has but twenty-eight days clear,
And twenty-nine in each leap year.'

III.

		BE	AE
1.	7 January 2002	7.1.2002	1.7.2002
2.	12 November 2003	12.11.2003	11.12.2003
3.	11 December 2006	11.12.2006	12.11.2006
4.	5 April 2005	5.4.2005	4.5.2005

IV. **1.** 31 December - **2.** 14 February - **3.** 5 November - **4.** 17 March - **5.** 26 December

V. **1.** 'quarter past twelve in the morning' - **2.** 'quarter to four in the (early) morning' - **3.** 'twenty-five past four in the afternoon' - **4.** 'twenty past nine at night' - **5.** 'ten to four in the (early) morning' - **6.** 'twenty-five to seven in the evening'

47 Practice

(See also Fast Track, Modules 2B, 4A-4E, 9A, 13A, 13B, 19A, 19B; The Business World, Modules 6E, 11A)

I.

form of transport	people
air	pilot, stewardess
rail	porter, ticket collector
road	chauffeur, conductor (in a bus)
sea	captain, purser

II. **1.** ... accelerator, ... brake ... clutch. - **2.** ... boot. - **3.** ... handbrake ... .- **4.** ... indicator ... - **5.** ... windscreen wipers. - **6.** ... aerial. - **7.** ... seatbelt. - **8.** ... bumper ... bumper?

III. After passing through a **security check**, ... , we could go into the **departure lounge**. The first thing we did was to buy some perfume in the **duty free shop**. Then we sat down near a television **screen** and ...

flight to be called. Fortunately the plane **took off** on time ... . We went to the **baggage reclaim** area... . After a few minutes our stuff appeared on the **conveyor belt**. We put everything on a **trolley**, passed quickly through **customs** and took the first **taxi** we could find.

IV. **1.** A 'van' is a small vehicle for transporting small items. A 'lorry' is much larger. - **2.** A 'bus' is used for short journeys. A 'coach' is more comfortable. - **3.** A car has four 'wheels'. You use a 'steering wheel' to steer the car. - **4.** You put your luggage in a 'boot'. Under the 'bonnet' is the engine.

48 Practice

I. **1.** I had a ride on my friend's motorbike. - **2.** In the afternoon we had a walk into the village. - **3.** They had a beer before they went out. - **4.** She had a dance with her father first.

II. **1.** They decided to close one of the factories. - **2.** Let's break for five minutes (or: for a while), shall we? - **3.** She wants (= would like) a day's holiday next week. - **4.** He breathed in deeply and jumped into the swimming pool.

III. **1.** She made a good **impression** ... . - **2.** Can I make a **suggestion**? ... . - **3.** ... I didn't make a **sound**. - **4.** They made an **effort** ... .

IV. **1.** I can give ... . - **2.** ... Can you give ... ? - **3.** She gave ... . - **4.** ... Would you like to give ... ?

V. **2.** Why do you always <u>take</u> offence when I make a suggestion?

49 Practice

I. **1.** ... rack and ruin. - **2.** ... rough and ready ... . - **3.** ... here and there. - **4.** ... on and off ... . - **5.** ... back and forth ... !

II. **1.** d. - **2.** c. - **3.** a. - **4.** e. - **5.** b.

III. **1.** e. - **2.** a. - **3.** h. - **4.** f. - **5.** b. - **6.** g. - **7.** d. - **8.** c.

50 Practice

I. **1.** affect - **2.** lend - **3.** postpone - **4.** inspected - **5.** delayed - **6.** interested 7. job - **8.** journey - **9.** living - **10.** measurements - **11.** rise - **12.** receipt

II. **1.** a) - **2.** c) - **3.** c) - **4.** c) - **5.** a) - **6.** a) - **7.** a) - **8.** c)

Wordlist

A

A (*Advanced*) levels 12	*entspricht etwa dem Abitur*
abbreviation 29	Abkürzung
absent-minded 37	zerstreut, geistesabwesend
accelerator 47	Gaspedal
accountant 25	Buchhalter/in
acquaintance 16	Bekanntschaft, Bekannte(r)
actually 15	eigentlich
ad (*informal*) 2	Anzeige (*Werbung*)
admiration 5	Bewunderung
to admire 5	bewundern
adventurous 37	abenteuerlustig, waghalsig, kühn
advertisement 2	Anzeige (*Werbung*)
advice 50	Rat(schlag)
to advise 5	raten, empfehlen, beraten
advisor 5	Berater, Ratgeber
aerial (*BE*) 47	Antenne
afterthought 9	nachträglicher Einfall
aggressive 37	aggressiv, angriffslustig
to agree 5	übereinstimmen, einwilligen, zustimmen
air conditioning 21	Klimaanlage
alarm clock 13	Wecker
amazed 38	erstaunt, verblüfft
amusing 37	lustig, amüsant
ankle 3	(Fuß)Knöchel
annoyed 38	verärgert
answerphone 36	Anrufbeantworter
ant 45	Ameise
anxious 38	besorgt, unruhig
appendicitis 19	Blinddarmentzündung
apple fritters 11	*etwa*: Apfelpfannkuchen
apple pie 17	*etwa*: Apfelkuchen
application 2	Bewerbung
application form 25	Bewerbung(sformular)
apprehensive 38	angstvoll, voller Befürchtungen

archery 41	Bogenschießen
architect 25	Architekt/in
armchair 22	Sessel
arson 27	Brandstiftung
art 44	Kunst
the arts 44	die schönen Künste
articulate 37	fähig, sich klar und deutlich ausdrücken zu können
artist 44	Künstler/in (*insbes.* Maler/in)
artiste 44	Artist/in, Sänger/in, Tänzer/in
asparagus 17	Spargel
assault 27	tätlicher Angriff, Körperverletzung
assertiveness 25	Durchsetzungsvermögen
autumn (*BE*) 14	Herbst
available 21	verfügbar, vorhanden
away with, to do ~ 31	abschaffen
axe 13	Axt

B

BA (*Bachelor of Arts*) 12	*erster akademischer Grad in den Geisteswissenschaften an angelsächsischen Universitäten*
back and forth 49	hin und her
back to front 49	falsch herum (*Kleidungsstück*)
bad-tempered 38	schlecht gelaunt, übellaunig
baffled 38	verblüfft
to bake 17	backen
to bar 34	ausschließen, Eintritt verwehren
barrel 8	Fass
bashful 37	scheu, schüchtern, verlegen
bat 41	(Kricket)Schläger
bathroom 22	Badezimmer
beans 17	Bohnen
to become 15	werden
bedroom 22	Schlafzimmer
bee 45	Biene
beef 17	Rindfleisch
belongings 27	Besitz, Habe

belt 6	Gürtel
bill 11, 14	Rechnung (*BE*); Geldschein (*AE*)
biology 12	Biologie
biro 36	Kugelschreiber
biscuits (*BE*) 8, 14	Kekse
bits and bobs 49	Krimskrams, Kleinkram
bitter 17	*dunkle engl. Biersorte*
blister 19	Blase (*Haut*)
blouse 6	Bluse
boastful 37	prahlerisch, überheblich
to boil 17	kochen, sieden
bonnet (*BE*) 14, 47	Motor-, Kühlerhaube
to book (a table) 11	(einen Tisch) reservieren
bookshelf 22	Bücherregal
boot (*BE*) 14, 47	Kofferraum
bored 38	gelangweilt
to borrow 30, 50	(aus)leihen
bottle 8	Flasche
bowl 8	Schüssel, Schale
box 8	Schachtel
braces 6	Hosenträger
brake 47	Bremse
brass 32	(Blech)Blasinstrumente
to break off 31	abbrechen, beenden
to break up 16	sich trennen
bribery 27	Bestechung
bright 37	aufgeweckt, gescheit, klug
to bring 50	(her)bringen
bruise 19	Quetschung, blauer Fleck
BSc (*Bachelor of Science*) 12	*Erster akademischer Grad in den Naturwissenschaften an angelsächsischen Universitäten*
bucket 8	Eimer
buckle 15	Schnalle
bumper 47	Stoßstange
bunk beds 22	Etagenbett
burglary 27	Einbruch(sdiebstahl)
butcher 25	Metzger/in
buttercup 45	Butterblume

C

calculator 36	Rechenmaschine, Taschenrechner
calendar 50	Kalender
calm 37, 38	ruhig, friedlich, gelassen
camp site 21	Campingplatz
can 8	Dose, Büchse
Carinthia 10	Kärnten
carrots 17	Karotten
carton 8	Becher, Tetrapack
cauliflower 17	Blumenkohl
cause 50	Ursache, Grund
charismatic 37	charismatisch, persönliche Ausstrahlung
cheeky 37	frech, unverschämt, dreist
cheerful 38	froh, gut aufgelegt
chef 15	Koch/Köchin (Küchenchef/in)
chemistry 12	Chemie
chess 20	Schach
chest 19	Brust
chest of drawers 22	Kommode
chicken 17	Huhn
chilly 18	kühl, frostig
chives 17	Schnittlauch
to chop 13	(zer)hacken, (*Holz*) spalten
chubby 39	mollig, pausbäckig
cinnamon 17	Zimt
to clash 34	zusammenstoßen, kollidieren, kämpfen
classic 44	klassisch (*im Sinne von typisch*)
classical 44	klassisch (*im Sinne von traditionell*)
claw 45	Kralle, Klaue
clothes 6	Kleider, Kleidung
club 20	Kreuz (*Kartenspiel*)
clutch 47	Kupplung
coat 6	Mantel
coffee grinder 13	elektr. Kaffeemühle
collar 6	Kragen
compensation 24	Entschädigung
complacent 38	selbstzufrieden, selbstgefällig

to complain 18	sich beschweren, klagen
compliment slip 36	Empfehlungskärtchen
conceited 37	eingebildet
conductor 32	Dirigent/in, Chorleiter/in
conference facilities 21	Konferenzräume
confident 37	zuversichtlich
confidential 50	vertraulich
conservatory 22	Wintergarten
considerate 37	rücksichtsvoll, aufmerksam, zuvorkommend
constipated 19	verstopft (*med.*)
container 8	Behälter
content 8	Inhalt
contented 38	zufrieden
contract 24	Vertrag
cookies (*AE*) 14	Kekse
cordless phone 43	schnurloses Telefon
corked 11	nach Korken schmeckend (*Wein*)
cough 19	Husten
court 3	Tennisplatz
cover note 24	Deckungszusage, vorläufiger Versicherungsschein
creative 37	kreativ, schöpferisch
critic 15	Kritiker/in
crocus 45	Krokus
cupboard 22	Schrank, Buffet
current 15	aktuell
current account 30	Girokonto
to cut 34	verringern, reduzieren

D

daffodil 45	Narzisse
daisy 45	Gänseblümchen
dandelion 45	Löwenzahn
Danube 10	Donau
daring 37	wagemutig, risikofreudig
date stamp 36	Tages-, Poststempel
debit 30	Soll, Lastschrift
debts 30	Schulden

degree 12	Grad, Abschluß (*Bachelor, Magister, Doktor*)
deliberately 37	vorsätzlich, absichtlich
dentist 25	Zahnärztin/Zahnarzt
deposit account 30	Sparkonto
desk 22	Schreibtisch
dessert 11	Nachspeise
detached house 22	freihstehendes Haus
diamond 20	Karo (*Kartenspiel*)
diary 36, 50	Terminkalender
dimple 39	Grübchen
dining room 22	Eßzimmer
dinner jacket (*BE*) 6	Smoking
direct debit 30	Einzugsauftrag
director 32	Regisseur/in
to disagree 5	nicht übereinstimmen, nicht einverstanden sein
disappointed 38	enttäuscht
to discourage 5	entmutigen, abraten
to dish out 31	verteilen
dishwasher 13	Spülmaschine
disillusioned 38	desillusioniert, ernüchtert, enttäuscht
to distribute 31	verteilen
dizzy 19	schwindelig, benommen
doctor 25	Ärztin/Arzt
doctoral degree 15	Promotion
domineering 37	tonangebend, herrisch, beherrschend
to donate 15	spenden, stiften
double fault 3	Doppelfehler (*Tennis*)
double glazing 22	Doppelverglasung
down 38	niedergeschlagen
down-to-earth 37	rein sachlich, nüchtern
to draw (*a game*) 3	unentschieden spielen
drawing pin 36	Reißzwecke
dress 6	Kleid
to dress 5	anziehen, (be)kleiden
to dress up 31	sich schick anziehen
dressmaker 25	Schneider/in
drill 13	Bohrmaschine

to drop in 31	vorbeikommen, hereinschauen
to drop off 31	einnicken
dyed 39	gefärbt (*Haar*)

E

economic 50	wirtschaftlich, Wirtschafts-
economical 50	sparsam, wirtschaftlich (*Verbrauch*)
edgy 38	nervös, gereizt, angespannt
electric 13	elektrisch
electric blanket 13	elektrische Heizdecke
electrical appliances 13	Elektrogeräte
electrical engineer 13	Elektroingenieur/in
electrical equipment 13	elektrisches Zubehör
electrical goods 13	Elektrogeräte
electrician 25	Elektriker/in
emotional 37	emotional, gefühlsbetont
to encourage 5	ermutigen, aufmuntern
engine 47	Motor
engineer 25	Ingenieur/in
enthusiastic 37	begeistert, leidenschaftlich
envelope 36	Briefumschlag
equipment 3	Ausrüstung, Ausstattung
eventually 15	schließlich, endlich, am Ende
exam 12	Prüfung
exhaust 47	Auspuff
expenses 30	Aufwendungen, Auslagen
expensive 30	teuer
extension lead 36	Verlängerungskabel

F

faint 19	schwindelig (*nahe einer Ohnmacht*)
to fail an exam 12	durch eine Prüfung fallen
fall (*AE*) 14	Herbst
to fall out 16, 31	sich streiten, sich zanken
fax machine 36	Faxgerät
fed up, to be ~ with sth 38	die Nase voll haben von etwas
filing cabinet 36	Aktenschrank, -regal

fine arts 44	bildende Künste
to finish school 12	die Schule beenden
first and foremost 49	zu allererst
first floor 14	1. Stock (*BE*); Erdgeschoss (*AE*)
flexitime 25	Gleitzeit
fond, to be ~ of 20	mögen, gern haben
food processor 13	Küchenmaschine
foot/feet (= 12 inches) 29	Fuß (*Maßeinheit*)
football match 3	Fußballspiel
football pitch 3	Fußballplatz, -feld
football shirt 3	Fußballtrikot
forgery 27	Fälschung
form 30	Formblatt, Formular, Vordruck
formula 30	Formel (*z.B. Mathematik*)
freckles 39	Sommersprossen
freezer 13	Gefrierschrank
fridge (*informal*) 2	Kühlschrank
fringe 39	Pony(frisur)
fruit 17	Obst
frustrated 38	frustriert, enttäuscht
to fry 17	braten, backen
full board 21	Vollpension
fully-comprehensive insurance 24	Vollkaskoversicherung
furious 38	wütend

G

game 3	Spiel
gas (*AE*) 14	Benzin
GCSEs (*General Certificate of Secondary Education*) 12	*entspricht etwa der Mittleren Reife*
gear lever 47	Schalthebel
geography 12	Erdkunde
gerbil 45	Wüstenspringmaus
to get 15	bekommen
to get down to 31	sich machen an, in Angriff nehmen
to get on (well) 16	(gut) miteinander auskommen
to get on to 31	sich in Verbindung setzen mit
to get on with 31	mit jmdm. zurechtkommen, auskommen

gift 15	Geschenk
ginger 17	Ingwer
to give up 31	aufhören, aufgeben
glass 8	Glas
glove compartment 47	Handschuhfach
gloves 6	Handschuhe
glue 36	Klebstoff
to go for 31	losgehen auf
to go to (*school, college, university*) 12	zur (*Schule, College, Universität*) gehen
goggles 41	Schutzbrille
good, to be ~ at 12	(in einer Sache) gut sein
grape 17	Weintraube
to grill 17	grillen
guest house 21	Pension
guillotine 36	Papierschneidemaschine
guinea pig 45	Meerschweinchen
gullible 37	leichtgläubig, naiv
gymnasium 15	Turnhalle

H

hairdresser 25	Friseurin/Friseur
hairdryer 13	Fön
half board 21	Halbpension
hall 22	Diele, Eingangshalle
handbrake 47	Handbremse
handy 15	praktisch
hang-gliding 20	Gleitschirmfliegen
hangover 40	„Kater“
Hanover 10	Hannover
happy ending 15	Happyend („glückliches Ende“)
harpsichord 32	Cembalo
headache 19	Kopfschmerzen
headed paper 36	Briefpapier mit Briefkopf
heartbroken 38	mit gebrochenem Herzen, in tiefem Schmerz
hedgehog 45	Igel
heel 6	Absatz (*Schuh*)

herbs 17	Kräuter
here and there 49	überall, da und dort
Hesse 10	Hessen
highly-strung 37	reizbar, überempfindlich
history 12	Geschichte
to hit it off 16	gut miteinander auskommen
hole punch 36	Locher
holidays 21	Ferien
homesick, to be ~ 38	Heimweh haben
hood (*AE*) 14	Motor-, Kühlerhaube
hoover 13	Staubsauger
hospitable 37	gastlich, gastfreundlich
humiliated 38	gedemütigt, erniedrigt
hump 15	Buckel

I

illegal 5	ungesetzlich, unrechtmäßig, illegal
illegible 5	unleserlich, unlesbar
impatient 5, 37	ungeduldig, übereifrig
in advance 11	im Voraus
inch (= 2.54 cm) 29	Zoll (*Maßeinheit*)
indicator 47	Blinker
inefficient 5	unwirksam, wirkungslos, unwirtschaftlich, unrentabel
to invent 31	erfinden
irregular 5	unregelmäßig, ungebräuchlich, abweichend
irritable 38	reizbar, ungeduldig
to itch 19	jucken

J

jacket 6	Jacke, Jackett
jam 1, 8	Marmelade
jar (*eg of jam*) 8	Glas
javelin 41	Wurfspieß
jug 8	Krug, Kanne

K

kettle 13	Wasserkocher
kitchen 22	Küche
knitting 20	Stricken

L

laces 6	Schnürsenkel
ladybird 45	Marienkäfer
lager 17	*engl. helle Biersorte mit Kohlensäure; wird kalt getrunken*
Lake Constance 10	Bodensee
lamb 17	Lamm(fleisch)
lamb chops 1	Lammkottelets
landing 22	Flur (*im 1. Stock*)
last but not least 15	zu guter Letzt, nicht zu vergessen
lawn 22, 45	Rasen
lawyer 25	Rechtsanwältin/Rechtsanwalt
leadership 25	Führungsqualitäten
to leave school 12	die Schule beenden
leek 17	Lauch, Porree
legal 5	gesetz-, rechtmäßig, legal
legible 5	lesbar, leserlich, deutlich
lemonade 8	Zitronenlimonade
to lend 30, 50	(ver)leihen
lessons (to have ~) 12	Unterricht (haben)
lettuce 17	Kopfsalat
liability 24	Verpflichtung, Haftung, Haftpflicht
liable 24	verpflichtet, verantwortlich, haftbar
light-headed 38	schwindelig
light switch 47	Lichtschalter
lights 47	Scheinwerfer
to lock 5	zuschließen, absperren
lonely 38	einsam
to look after 31	sich kümmern um
to look up 31	aufwärts gehen
to look up to 31	zu jmdm. aufsehen, bewundern
to look for 31	suchen

lorry (*BE*) 14	Lastwagen
lose (*a game*) 3	(*ein Spiel*) verlieren
lounge 22	Wohnzimmer
love 35	Null (*Tennis*)
Lower Saxony 10	Niedersachsen
loyal 37	loyal, (pflichtge)treu

M

mad 14	verrückt (*BE*); wütend (*AE)*
main course 11	Hauptgericht (*Essen*)
to make a claim 24	Anspruch erheben auf
to make up 16	(*Streit*) beilegen
to make up 31	erfinden
malicious 37	boshaft, böswillig
mane 45	Mähne
mansion 21	stattlicher Bau, Herrenhaus
manslaughter 27	Totschlag
manual worker 25	Arbeiter/in
matches 8	Streichhölzer
mate (*informal*) 16	Kamerad, Kumpel
maternity leave 25	Mutterschaftsurlaub
maths 12	Mathe(matik)
to mature 24	fällig werden (*Versicherung*)
meaning 15	Bedeutung, Sinn
measurements 29	Maßangaben, Maße, Abmessungen
measure 29	Maßeinheit
meat 11, 17	Fleisch
mechanic 25	Mechaniker/in
menu 11	Speisekarte, Speisenfolge
miserable 38	elend, unglücklich
mixed-up 38	verwirrt
mobile (phone) 15, 43	Handy, Mobiltelefon
modest 37	bescheiden, anspruchslos, zurückhaltend
mole 39	Muttermal
mole 45	Maulwurf
monthly statement 30	Kontoauszug
to mow 45	(ab)mähen

mug (*eg of coffee*) 8	große Tasse, „Haferl“
murder 27	Mord
mustard 17	Senf
mutton 17	Hammelfleisch

N

nail 13	Nagel
narrow-minded 37	engstirnig
negligent 24	fahrlässig
net 3	Netz
nice 15	sympatisch, nett
niece 16	Nichte
nil 35	Null (*Football, Rugby*)
no-claim discount 24	Schadenfreiheitsrabatt
nostalgic 38	wehmütig, voll Sehnsucht
nostrils 45	Nüstern
notebook 36	Notizbuch
nought 35	Null
nursery school 12	Kindergarten, Vorschule
nutmeg 17	Muskatnuß

O

oar 41	Ruder
obese 39	fettleibig
to occur 24	sich ereignen, geschehen
oh 35	Null (*Telefonnummern, Kontonummern*)
on and off 49	gelegentlich, hin und wieder
onion 17	Zwiebel
to open 5	öffnen, aufmachen
opener 5	Öffner
ordinary 15	gewöhnlich
to be out and about 49	unterwegs, auf den Beinen sein
oven 13	Backofen
overcooked 11	verkocht (*Essen*)

P

pack 8	Packung
packet 8	Schachtel, Packung
pane 22	(Fenster)Scheibe
pantry 22	Vorrats-, Speisekammer
paper clip 36	Büroklammer
parachuting 20	Fallschirmspringen
paranoid 38	paranoid, unter Verfolgungswahn leiden
parsley 17	Petersilie
parting 39	Scheitel
pass 15	Passierschein
to pass an exam 12	eine Prüfung bestehen
passport 15	Pass
patient 5	geduldig, ausdauernd
pavement (*BE*) 14	Bürgersteig
paw 45	Pfote, Tatze
pawn 20	Bauer (*Schachspiel*)
to pay by cheque 11	mit Scheck (be)zahlen
to pay in cash 30	bar zahlen
to pay in instalments 30	in Raten zahlen
to pay interest 30	Zinsen zahlen
pay rise 25	Gehaltserhöhung
pear 17	Birne
pencil 36	Bleistift
percussion 32	Schlaginstrumente
performing arts 44	darstellende Kunst
personal 50	persönlich, privat
personnel 50	Personal, Belegschaft
petrified 38	erstarrt, versteinert
petrol (*BE*) 14	Benzin
photcopier 36	Fotokopierer
physics 12	Physik
pigeon 45	Taube
pillow 22	Kopfkissen
pineapple 17	Ananas
pint (a ~, half a ~) 8	*Maßeinheit für Flüssigkeiten in GB*
plait 39	Zopf

pliers 13	Kneifzange
plug 36	Stecker
plumber 25	Klempner/in, Installateur/in
pneumonia 19	Lungenentzündung
poison 15	Gift
pole vault 41	Stabhochsprung
policy 24	(Versicherungs)police, Versicherungsschein
to pollute 5	verunreinigen, beschmutzen
pollution 5	Verschmutzung, Verunreinigung
porch 22	überdachter Hauseingang
pork 17	Schweinefleisch
potato (*pl* -oes) 17	Kartoffeln
potato chips 14	Pommes Frites (*BE*); Chips (*AE*)
pound (*lb*) 29	Pfund (*Maßeinheit*)
premium 24	(Versicherungs)Prämie
price 50	Preis, Kosten
primary school 12	Grundschule
principal 50	Schulleiter
principle 50	Prinzip
printer 36	Drucker
prize 50	Auszeichnung, Preis
to probe 15	untersuchen
products liability 24	Produkthaftung
profession 25	Beruf
programme, TV ~ (*BE*) 14 program (*AE*) 14	Fernsehsendung
promotion 15	Werbung
public liability 24	*Haftung bei Verletzung der sog. Verkehrssicherungspflicht (z.B. in öffentl. Gebäuden)*
to put up with 31	tolerieren, akzeptieren
pyjamas (*BE*) 6, 14 pajamas (*AE*) 14	Schlafanzug

R

rack and ruin, to go to ~ 49	verfallen
racket 3	(Tennis-)Schläger
radiator 47	Kühler
to raise 50	(hoch)heben
rambling 20	Wandern
rape 27	Vergewaltigung
rash 19	Hautausschlag
rash 37	hastig, vorschnell, unbesonnen
raspberry 17	Himbeere
raw plug 13	Dübel
reason 50	Grund, Ursache, Anlaß
receipt 30	Quittung, Beleg
to reduce 5	verringern, vermindern, reduzieren
reduction 5	Verringerung, Verminderung, Reduktion
redundant, to be made ~ 25	den Arbeitsplatz verlieren
refrigerator 2	Kühlschrank
regular 5	regelmäßig, geordnet, ordentlich
regular hours 25	geregelte Arbeitszeit
to rehearse 15, 32	proben, einüben
relaxed 38	entspannt
to repeat a year 12	ein Jahr wiederholen (*Schule*)
resentful 38	beleidigt, eingeschnappt
to resit an exam 12	eine Prüfung wiederholen
retail 25	Einzelhandel
retirement 25	Ruhestand
to revise 12	überarbeiten, revidieren, *hier*: lernen
to ripen 24	reifen lassen
to rise 50	aufgehen, aufstehen, steigen
to rob 27	(aus)rauben
robin 45	Rotkehlchen
rosemary 17	Rosmarin
rough and ready 49	schlicht, einfach, lieblos zusammengeschustert
rowing 41	Rudern
rubber 36	Radiergummi
rubber band 36	Gummiring
ruler 36	Lineal

S

sandpaper 13	Sand-, Schmirgelpapier
sausage 17	Wurst
saw 13	(Hand)Säge
scales 36	(Brief)Waage
scar 39	Narbe
scared, to be ~ 28, 38	Angst haben
sceptical 37, 38	skeptisch, zweifelnd
school (to go to ~) 12	(zur) Schule (gehen)
school-leaving exams (to take ~) 12	Abschlußprüfung an der Schule (ablegen)
scissors 36	Schere
score 3	Punktzahl, Spielergebnis, Spielstand
screw 13	Schraube
screwdriver 13	Schraubenzieher
seatbelt 47	Sicherheitsgurt
secondary school 12	höhere Schule
self-catering accommodation 21	Unterbringung mit Selbstverpflegung
self-confident 37	selbstsicher
sellotape 36	Tesafilm, Klebestreifen
semi-detached house 22	Doppelhaushälfte
sensible 37	vernünftig
sentimental 38	empfindsam, gefühlvoll
to serve 3	aufschlagen (*Tennis*)
service 11	Bedienung
set 3	Satz (*Tennis*)
to set up 31	vorbereiten, planen
setee 22	Sofa, Polsterbank
sharpener 36	Anspitzer
shed 22	Schuppen
shepherd's pie 1	*Auflauf aus Hackfleisch und Kartoffelbrei*
shifts, to work ~ 25	Schichtarbeit
shirt 6	Hemd
shoplifting 27	Ladendiebstahl
short 29	klein (gewachsen)
to shortlist 25	in die engere Wahl ziehen
shot put 41	Kugelstoßen

shuttlecock 3	Federball
sidewalk (*AE*) 14	Bürgersteig
sister-in-law 16	Schwägerin
size 29	(Kleider)Größe
skilled 25	ausgebildet, Fach-
skirt 6	Rock
sleeve 6	Ärmel
sleeveless jumper 15	Pullunder
slim 39	schlank, schmächtig, schmal
slip-on-shoe 15	Slipper
slipper 15	Hausschuh
snail 45	Schnecke
snowdrop 45	Schneeglöckchen
socket 36	Steckdose
socks 6	Socken, Strümpfe
soft drink 17	alkoholfreies Getränk
sooner or later 49	früher oder später
sore 19	entzündet, wund
sore throat 19	Halsschmerzen
South Tyrol 10	Südtirol
spade 20	Pik (*Kartenspiel*)
Spaniard 10	Spanier/in
Spanish 10	spanisch
spanner 13	Schraubenschlüssel
sparrow 45	Spatz
speechless 38	sprachlos
to spend 15	ausgeben
spices 17	Gewürze
spinach 17	Spinat
spirit level 13	Wasserwaage
spirits 17	*hochprozentige alkoholische Getränke*
to sprain 19	verrenken, verstauchen
to stand in for 31	einspringen
to stand out 31	herausragen, hervorstechen (*Wertung*)
standing order 30	Dauerauftrag
stapler 36	Hefter, Tacker
starter 11	Vorspeise

stationary 50	(fest)stehend, ruhend
stationery 50	Schreib-, Papierwaren
to stay up 31	aufbleiben
to steal 27	stehlen
steeplechase 41	Hindernislauf
steering wheel 47	Lenkrad
stepfather 16	Stiefvater
to stick up for 31	eintreten für
stiff 19	steif, starr
stomach ache 19	Bauchschmerzen
stone (*st*) (= 14 pounds) 29	*britische Maßeinheit*
stool 22	Hocker, Schemel
stout 39	stämmig, kräftig, stark
string 32	Saiteninstrument, Streicher
stroke 19	Schlaganfall
strong-willed 37	willensstark
study 22	Arbeitszimmer
sty 19	Gerstenkorn (*med.*)
subjects (school ~) 12	Unterrichtsfächer
to submit 24	(*Anspruch*) erheben
subway 14	Unterführung (*BE*); U-Bahn (*AE*)
suit 6	Anzug, Kostüm
surname 33	Familien-, Zuname
Swede 10	Schwedin/Schwede
Swedish 10	schwedisch
to switch on 31	an-, einschalten
swivel chair 36	Drehstuhl, -sessel
sympathetic 15	mitfühlend

T

to take 50	(hin)bringen
to take exams 12	Prüfungen machen/ablegen
talented 37	talentiert, begabt
tall 29	groß (gewachsen), hoch
television 13	Fernseher
terraced house 22	Reihenhaus
tests (to do ~) 12	Prüfungen, Tests (schreiben, ablegen)
theft 27	Diebstahl

third-party, fire and theft insurance 24	Teilkaskoversicherung
thrilled 38	hocherfreut, freudig erregt
thumb 28	Daumen
thyme 17	Thymian
thyroid 19	Schilddrüse
tie 6	Kravatte
tied up 39	zusammengebunden (*Haare*)
timber 21	Nutzholz, Balken
time-share apartment 21	*Wohnung auf Timesharing-Basis*
tin (*eg of beans*) 8	Blechdose, Konservenbüchse
tip 11	Trinkgeld
tire (*AE*) 14	Reifen
tool 13	Werkzeug
toothache 19	Zahnschmerzen
touchy 38	empfindlich, reizbar, heikel
tough 11	zäh (*Fleisch*)
towels 22	Handtücher
train spotting 20	Zugnummern sammeln
to train to become 12	eine Ausbildung machen/absolvieren um ... zu werden
tray 36	Ablagekorb
tray 40	Tablett
trombone 32	Posaune
trousers 6	Hose
truck (*AE*) 14	Lastwagen
trunk (*AE*) 14	Kofferraum
tube (*eg of toothpaste*) 8	Tube
tulip 45	Tulpe
Turk 10	Türkin/Türke
Turkish 10	türkisch
to turn over 30	umdrehen, umblättern
turnover 30	Umsatz
twenties, sb in their ~ 15	Twen
tyre (*BE*) 14	Reifen

U

undercooked	11	nicht gar (*Essen*)
underground parking	21	Tiefgarage
undertaker	15	Leichenbestatter/in
to undress	5	ausziehen, entkleiden
to unlock	5	aufschließen, aufsperren
up and down	49	auf und ab
Upper Franconia	10	Oberfranken
utility room	22	Wirtschaftsraum

V

VAT (*value added tax*)	11	Mehrwertsteuer
veal	17	Kalbfleisch
vegetables	11, 17	Gemüse
versatile	37	vielseitig (begabt)
vest	14	Unterhemd (*BE*); Weste (*AE*)
vet	25	Tierärztin/Tierarzt
vintage car	15	Oldtimer
to visit	12	besuchen
void	24	ungültig
voluntary excess	24	(freiwillige) Selbstbeteiligung
vulgar	15	ordinär

W

waist	29	Taille
waistcoat	6	Weste
to wait up	31	wachbleiben
waiter	11	Ober
wardrobe	22	Garderobe, Kleiderschrank
wastepaper bin	36	Papierkorb
weak	19	schwach
wheels	47	Reifen
whiskers	45	Schnurrhaare
to win (*a game*)	3	(*ein Spiel*) gewinnen
windscreen wiper	47	Scheibenwischer
to wine and dine	49	(zum Essen) ausführen

to wipe out 31	ausradieren, zerstören
woodwind 32	(Holz)Blasinstrument
to work for 12	arbeiten für
to work freelance 25	freischaffend arbeiten
wrinkled 39	runzlig, faltig
to write 5	schreiben
writer 5	Schreiber, Schriftsteller
writer's address 9	Absender

Y

youth hostel 21	Jugendherberge